What others are saying about this book:

"After eighteen years of raising my children, I was startled to learn several critical things about them and my relationships to them through this book. I wish I had read it years ago."

John Cown, author of *Small Decencies*

"So much psycho babble on the newsstand ... so much common sense in *Figuring Kids Out*! Stand aside self esteem gurus, Sandra Merwin has just told us everything we need to know. Get it, read it, use it."

Michele Halliday, School Counselor

"Any parents who want to nurture and esteem their child will gain real insights from this book. They will understand what motivates their child. This new understanding will help them to be much better parents and get better results when they need to guide and coach their child to more appropriate behavior. The book is easy to read, easy to implement and filled with specific suggestions."

Candance Hennekens, author of *Healing Your Life*

"I continue to be impressed with Sandra's wisdom and insight and her understanding of human issues across generations. *Figuring Kids Out* is written in an engaging style which makes learning about oneself and others a rich experience. I wish I'd had this book when my children were young."

Anne Graves, University of St Thomas Manager of Counseling and Career Services for Business and Industry

"This behavior style knowledge should be required of every parent and teacher. It's essential to building a child's self esteem. *Figuring Kids Out* is valuable for anyone wanting a fresh approach to building children's self-esteem and honoring diversity."

Peggy Jenkins, author of *The Joyful Child*

FIGURING KIDS OUT:

A Guide to Understanding Children

SANDRA J. MERWIN

TigerLily Press
Minnetonka, Minnesota

Merwin, Sandra J.
    Figuring kids out : a guide to understanding children /
Sandra J. Merwin.
    p. cm.
    ISBN 0-9628522-1-X

    1. Child psychology. 2. Parent and child. 3. Child rearing.
I. Title.

    BF721.M4 1993   155.4
                                           QBI93-20087

10 9 8 7 6 5 4 3 2

Printed in the United States of America

In this book, female and male pronouns are used alternately
chapter by chapter. My examples are from my life and from the
stories parents and teachers have freely shared with me. The
details of examples have been changed in order to honor other's
boundaries and prevent identification.

To my mother, Jacqueline Jean Taylor Cook

Contents

ACKNOWLEDGEMENTS

I am deeply appreciative to the parents who shared their family joys and struggles with me.

I especially want to thank Chris and Joanne Kudrna, who asked the questions, and Anneliese Dilworth, who helped more than she knows.

INTRODUCTION

Several years ago, as I discussed the natural motivations of children, a colleague interrupted me to proclaim, "Sandra, you must write this down. Parents are desperate for information that will help them raise healthy, esteemed children." At the time, I thought he must be exaggerating.

Over the years, parents and teachers have continued to ask me about their children's behaviors. In August of 1991, when a friend called to ask about her daughter's tears, I complained about the amount of time I was spending with parents discussing their children's behaviors. "Then write it down so we can read it!" responded my caller.

So I did.

1

Why Children Behave as They Do

The Sacred Covenant: To love all the children
and nurture their spirits.

When parents tell of the first time they held their newborn children, both fathers and mothers report a sense of wonder at the small life. Parents often experience a miraculous new beginning in their own lives as they touch the tiny hands and miniature feet. Some mothers divulge they are overwhelmed with the desire to change the world to create a better place for the infant. Others disclose they are awed and frightened by the intense responsibility for the new soul.

Teachers often report similar feelings for their students; the feeling of responsibility for their charges, the excitement of new beginnings at the start of the school year, and the pride when they see a child begin to grow and change.

The majority of parents, teachers and adults have a deep commitment to raising healthy, whole children. This commitment may become difficult, even painful, when a parent or teacher doesn't understand a child's behavior. Imagine the mother who is totally committed to raising her daughter and yet the child refuses to cooperate about the simplest things like what clothes to wear. The mother may reason, "My child is bad. She won't do what I want her to do." When in fact, the child may be naturally motivated to do exactly what she is doing.

Teachers have similar experiences. Some children are so easy to teach and others seem to deliberately break the rules. "Why won't they behave?" is one of the most common questions. To answer this question, it is important to come to a more correct understanding about human behavior.

One of the most basic truths about human behavior is that all human beings are naturally motivated to get their needs met. Every human being has needs or requirements to support life. The most basic of these requirements are oxygen, water, food, sleep, clothing, shelter and safety. Abraham Maslow called these needs "existence needs." Maslow originally developed a *Hierarchy of Needs* to explain the natural drives people have to get their needs met. He found that needs could be divided into three categories: existence needs, such as survival and security; relationship needs, such as belonging and achievement; and fulfillment needs, which occur when an individual is motivated to learn and grow so he can realize his goals, potentials and life purpose.

Most adults have learned the socially accepted ways to get their needs met. Children are new to the rules of society and have not yet learned acceptable behaviors for getting their needs met. Adults have learned it is unacceptable to grab food from another person to meet their hunger needs, but young children, unless taught differently, will naturally take any food they see available if they are hungry.

All children are motivated to get their needs met. Obviously, children have existence needs. Because their bodies are growing, children have an incredible need for food, sleep and movement.

Any parent who has tried to talk to a hungry child knows that a hungry child is focused on his need to eat. When a child is hungry, he is naturally motivated or driven to get this existence need met.

Teachers report children are not motivated to learn when they come to school without breakfast. Of course not! A hungry child will be motivated to get his food needs met, just as a sleepy child will be motivated to meet his sleep needs.

The reason Maslow called his model the *Hierarchy of Needs* is because human needs are usually sequential. Before a child can be motivated to higher levels of needs such as relationship needs, he must have his existence needs met. This means for a child to be naturally focused on developing positive social skills, he must have his basic existence needs met.

Hungry children will not be naturally motivated to develop high-level social skills.

In fact, children's bodies have a variety of needs. As many parents and teachers know, children are naturally motivated to move. Movement, a strong natural drive in children, is necessary for muscle development and a healthy body. The child who doesn't have his movement needs met will be driven to fidget even though he may want to obey his teacher's admonishment to "sit still!"

Children are also naturally motivated to be vocal, as vocal indicators or talking can be a way to tell others what is needed. Before a child can focus his energy on higher levels of needs, such as achievement, he needs a variety of basic needs met: food, safety, attention, love and movement, just to name a few.

Although all human beings are motivated by similar needs, they use a range of different behaviors to get their needs met. Because a parent and child may use different behaviors, a parent may be totally confused as to why a child behaves the way he does. A parent who is easy-going and naturally uses pleasing behaviors to get his needs met, may be horrified to discover that his child takes the direct action of pushing his friends when his needs are blocked. If the parent doesn't understand the child's natural motivation for this direct, forceful behavior, the parent may be tempted to judge the child as bad, willful or purposefully causing trouble. When in fact, the child has not learned more productive ways to use his direct energies. The focus is to guide the child to learn productive ways to use his natural energies.

It sounds fairly simple; just understand the natural behaviors of children and then guide them toward using their natural energies in more productive ways. It's no surprise to most parents that this is not simple. It is demanding, rewarding, exhausting, exhilarating and downright hard work. What makes the situation of raising healthy, productive children even more complex is the parents' needs. Parents are naturally motivated to get their needs met also. Just as children are driven to meet their existence, relationship and fulfillment needs, so are their parents. Frequently the needs of the parent and the needs of the child are at cross purposes, such as:

A mother who has spent a hectic day at work may need to rest; but her child who has spent the whole day sitting at his desk in school may need to run and jump.

A father who works at night may need to sleep, but his child may need his attention and try to wake him.

A parent who is trying to catch a plane with a hungry child who wants to eat now.

A child may be motivated to talk all the time, while her parent may need private, quiet time.

The needs of the child and the needs of the adult parent or teacher may be totally different. This difference of needs often results in conflict and power struggles between the child and the adult.

To further complicate the parent-child or teacher-child relationship, the adult brings experiences from his own childhood which play an invisible yet powerful role in each situation. The adult's past experiences and his present beliefs form a reality which the child knows nothing about, for example:

A father who never felt supported by his own parents may invade the privacy of his son in his attempt to be supportive.

A mother who felt deprived of activities and opportunities may have her daughter registered for swimming, ballet, gymnastics and drama when she really wants free time.

Parents who grew up in a house where children were expected to be quiet may try to silence a child who is naturally motivated to talk all the time.

Parents who believe that sharing toys with others is important may have a child who prefers to play alone.

Parents who believe that children should always ask before taking action may have a child who usually takes action before thinking.

Anyone who's been around children for any length of time will discover that children are motivated for their own reasons, not the reasons of their parents or teachers. Parents and teachers can only motivate children for a brief period of time, because all true motivation is self-motivation. Through the use of explanations, threats and even punishment, parents and teachers are able to maintain control, but only momentarily, while they are standing over the children. It is impossible to motivate children to do what you want them to do unless they are naturally motivated to do it anyway. Rewards and punishments only work so long as they are in the range of the natural motivation of the child. The key is to understand the child's natural motivations and then place rewards and reprimands in the natural behavioral context that the child will understand.

The ultimate goal is for parents to understand their children's motivations and behaviors so they can create an environment where their children are self-motivated toward positive outcomes.

By understanding both the motivations and the behaviors of their children, parents and teachers have the opportunity to create new caring ways of esteeming the natural behaviors of children while guiding their behaviors toward more positive actions. In this way, adults can provide guidance so that children can be self-motivated to learn and develop in positive ways.

In reality, many children learn their natural behaviors are "bad." When a child believes he is naturally bad, he grows up with a hole in his self-esteem which can influence his behaviors as an adult. The experiences of childhood form the child's first understanding of his world. From these first experiences, children will try to make sense of their world. Each child experiences what happens when he cries or gets angry. Over time, the child forms a complex set of behaviors he uses to get his needs met. Out of these experiences and behaviors, each child creates his first understanding of who he is and how the world will treat him. Some children learn:
"What I do naturally isn't O.K. I'm bad."
"I'm not good at what I'm supposed to do."
"I get hit because I always do it wrong."
"I always have to hurry."
"I am loved."
"I am able to learn."

"My mother thinks I am stupid."
"I am always hungry."
"The world is a warm and loving place."
"I always do things wrong."
"I can make mistakes and be O.K."
"I get in trouble when I make mistakes."

The experiences of childhood become the foundation for the adult behaviors. Many children learn that their natural motivations are bad. In fact, children's natural motivations are natural. But because they are children, they often do not have the understanding of how to use appropriate behaviors to get their needs met. Instead of politely asking for something to eat when they are hungry, they may be demanding, whiny or crying; all behaviors motivated by hunger.

Adding to the confusion of not understanding children's motivation, many parents learned when they were children that "children must give up their own natural motivations." Many parents and teachers today still believe a child's spirit must be broken so that they can learn the right ways to behave.

Parents and teachers usually want what is best for the child. It's just that they often assume they naturally know what is best for a child from their viewpoint, not from the child's viewpoint. Each adult has a way of viewing the world, making choices and determining what is the best action to take in any situation. So it seems natural to assume that a parent or teacher will automatically know what is best for a child. In order to understand what is best for the child, it is critical to understand the child's natural behavioral drives.

The key question each parent needs to ask from an open frame of mind is: "What is best for this unique child?" In order to answer this question without a hidden agenda, a parent will first have to ask: "What do I want for this child?"

Most parents have deeply hidden agendas for their children that get in the way of determining "what is best for this unique child?" An honest parent may answer the question "What do I want for this child?" by saying:

"I want this child to have a better life than mine. A better life means this child will not get married as young as I did."

"I want my son to wait until he is at least 30 to start his family."

"My child will work in an office and make more money than I made."

"This child will focus more on a positive relationship with his wife than I have."

"I want my daughter to be more satisfied with her life than I am."

"This child will have a better relationship with his parents than I have."

"What is best for this unique child?" is a key question every parent will have to truthfully answer. Parents, who have struggled with this question, think it is best for each unique child:

• to be esteemed for his natural behaviors,

• to be nurtured for "who he is," not who his parents want him to be,

• to be respectfully guided toward the strengths of his behaviors,

• to be allowed the appropriate, natural consequences which result from the child's behavioral weaknesses,

• to be coached and guided away from his behavioral weaknesses so that he can gain more productive behaviors,

• to be encouraged to develop behavioral flexibility and adaptability, in order to deal effectively with life,

• to be allowed to make his own choices which are appropriate for his age and

• to be loved and nurtured for himself.

2

A Language to Honor Children

Parents, teachers and children can benefit from using a language that explains and honors children's natural behaviors. Usually children's natural behavioral strengths are seen as problems. Because children are new at life and have limited life experiences from which to develop more effective behaviors, they operate from the weaknesses of their natural behaviors. Natural behaviors have both strengths and weaknesses. It depends on how and in what situations a behavior is used. For example, a child who is motivated to talk will be praised for her verbal ability when she is responding to her teacher's questions. The same child using the same behavior may be reprimanded for talking when the teacher is explaining directions. Talking behavior elicits rewards and reprimands in different situations. For adults this may seem obvious, but for children who have limited experiences in various situations it may seem very confusing.

By using the language of behaviors to explain a child's behaviors, parents can: gain a new understanding of their child's unique natural energy, develop a clearer understanding of how the child views the world, accept and esteem their child's natural behaviors and direct the child to use more effective behaviors in different situations.

The language of behaviors breaks "how people act" into four categories. These four behavioral categories or styles are the behaviors people tend to use to get their needs met. The four styles of behavior are:

Behavior Category 1 **Active and Decisive**

Behavior Category 2 **Talkative and Animated**

Behavior Category 3 **Soft-Spoken and Cooperative**

Behavior Category 4   Cautious and Concerned About Doing Things Correctly

No one style is better than another; they are just different ways of behaving. Each style has both strengths and weaknesses. Most children have the ability to use behaviors from all four styles, even though they prefer one or two styles. These preferred behaviors are used more frequently and with a greater intensity. Parents usually recognize the style of their child's behavior early in the child's life with statements like:

"She was always active, even as a baby she couldn't sit still."

"He was always such a good, quiet child. He never gave me a bit of trouble."

"He's always been talkative. His report cards always had a comment from his teacher about how disruptive his talking was to the class."

"We have two children. One likes to spend time alone in her room. Her sister thinks being alone is punishment."

Like adults, children use different behaviors to get their needs met. An Active, Decisive child, operating out of her strengths, will make decisions quickly. She will probably be able to tell you exactly what she wants for lunch: "I want macaroni and cheese!" This same behavior can be seen as demanding and belligerent when she says: "I told you I want macaroni and cheese! I don't want this peanut butter sandwich!" A Talkative, Animated child's strength of high verbal ability may appear as a weakness to her parents, who hear a constant barrage of chatter. The Soft-spoken, Cooperative child's easy-going style may appear to be too passive for her parents' active lifestyle. And, the Cautious child's concern for doing things correctly may drive her parents to regard her as a perfectionist.

Parents are often baffled by the range of behavioral differences in siblings. In fact, many parents are dismayed to discover that their children do not have the same behavioral preferences of either parent. The parents who naturally enjoy quiet time without activity may be surprised to find their son wants to be active all of his waking hours. Parents who naturally want to be more involved with people may be surprised to discover their child likes playing quietly alone. Parents have to determine how to provide healthy self-esteem to a child who has behaviors which are clearly different than their own. Esteeming a child becomes even more difficult when the child, operating from her behavioral weaknesses, uses behaviors which are not acceptable.

Ideally, children need to be esteemed for their natural behaviors. In reality, most children experience a range of criticism for their natural behaviors. This criticism can vary from "put-downs" to abuse.

Put-downs can be direct or masquerade as humor. In fact, parents frequently tease their children about their behavioral characteristics by saying things like: "We call her motor mouth because she never stops talking."

Often through parental words and actions or through the child's interpretation of events, the child receives a "you should be different than you are" message. This type of message tells a child "not to be who she is." To get her needs met, she must give up her natural behaviors. The child may perceive her natural behaviors are wrong. Since these natural behaviors are part of the child's innate energy state, the child may come to experience herself as wrong. As the child grows, the behavioral differences become even clearer, as in the following situation:

Susan was an active, forceful child of four who could usually get adults to do what she wanted. One example of this frequently occurred at the dining room table as Susan told adult guests where to sit so she could sit by her favorite people. When Susan's mother tried to redirect her behavior by saying, "Susan, I want you to sit by your grandpa," Susan would shout "No!" and run from the room, leaving her mother embarrassed by her daughter's outburst. As Susan grew older, it became apparent that the results she wanted were usually more important than the people involved. Susan's mother, in an attempt to redirect Susan's behavior and to get Susan to understand that people are important, began comparing Susan to her sister,

Barbara. Barbara, who is five years older than Susan, was popular and outgoing when she was Susan's age. Susan's mother had the best of intentions. She wanted Susan to experience the good things her sister did, such as being voted a cheerleader. In her drive to teach Susan good social skills, her mother inadvertently sent the message to Susan that she wasn't valued for herself and she should be more like Barbara, who was the valued child. Susan's teachers told her mother that Susan frequently got irritated with the slowness of her classmates and would say things like, "I don't want to work with Mark. He's too slow." Susan's mother continually complained, "Susan, why are you so pushy and ill-mannered? I don't know where you get it. You're not like Barbara or me or your father. You should be more friendly and people-oriented. You'll never succeed in life if you don't learn to interact with people." The self-esteem damaging message Susan heard was "There is something wrong with you. You are different and that difference is bad. You are bad. To succeed in life you must be someone else."

It is important to point out that Susan's mother wasn't trying to purposely sabotage or lower the self-esteem of her daughter. Susan's mother wanted only the best for her child. Regardless of the intent, Susan grew up hearing the message: "You can't be who you are."

Every child is naturally motivated by her own needs-driven behavior. As much as children want to please their parents, all children are motivated by their own natural drives. When parents understand their children's natural behaviors, they can create an environment in which the child will be naturally motivated and esteemed.

The following checklist can be used to develop an understanding about the children in your life. To determine a child's natural behavioral style, just read through the descriptions. Put a check mark (√) next to the phrases which best describe the child's most common behaviors. As you read through the checklist, think about the most common behaviors you have observed.

BEHAVIORAL CHECKLIST[1]

Behavioral Category 1

___This child's preference is to communicate directly, quickly and to "tell" you what he or she wants.

___This child usually acts forcefully and boldly.

___This child can usually hold his or her ground with children his or her own age and even with some adults.

___This child is willing to take risks.

___This child is less dependent on help and often prefers to do things himself or herself.

Behavioral Category 2

___This child acts enthusiastically in most situations.

___This child may act spontaneous and carefree.

___This child finds others interesting and likes to be with people.

___This child acts in an outgoing manner and meets people easily.

___This child may be sentimental or have emotional highs and lows.

Behavioral Category 3

___This child acts patiently in most situations.

___This child usually listens more than talks.

___This child tends to be cooperative and usually gets along with others.

___This child is seen as easy-going.

___This child is less active toward trying new things and usually prefers the old or familiar.

1. For a more accurate assessment of your child's behavior, you can order Behavioral Profile Instruments from Carlson Learning Company. More information is in the Resource Section on page 119.

Behavioral Category 4

___This child is usually conscientious and concerned about doing things right.

___This child is cautious in most situations.

___This child likes to think things through.

___This child likes privacy and may like to play alone.

___This child is usually diplomatic.

Count up the number of checks (√) you made in each category. Determine which two categories have the most checks (√). Then read the descriptions about those two categories.

BEHAVIORAL CATEGORY 1

ACTIVE AND DECISIVE

Children with this behavioral style hate to lose. They may be somewhat demanding. They may ask a lot of questions. You may find them controlling the environment by "being the boss." Often they "tell" instead of ask. They are not afraid to barge in. These children are not afraid to fight for what they need or want. You can identify children with this style of behavior by their drive to do things quickly. In the classroom, these children may have trouble sitting for long periods of time. They have a natural energy that begs for activity. They need to take some type of action. If they are forced to sit still for long periods of time, they may resort to "stirring up" trouble.

BEHAVIORAL CATEGORY 2

TALKATIVE AND ANIMATED

Children with this behavioral style may like to show off or be the center of attention. They are able to get most people to listen to them talk. They usually make friends very easily and can be quite charming. They tend to want popularity and may be able to butter up others to get what they want. They know how to get attention and can easily talk to almost anyone. You can identify children with this behavioral style by their drive to talk or interact with all types of people. The most frequent comments you'll find on these children's report cards are: "Her talking frequently disrupts the class. If Sara would learn to do her own work, instead of discussing it with others, she would receive higher marks." "Jack always volunteers to answer questions." "Pat is good at contributing to the classroom discussions."

BEHAVIORAL CATEGORY 3

SOFT-SPOKEN AND COOPERATIVE

Children with this behavioral style probably dislike fighting. They prefer to cooperate with others. They tend to come across as soft-spoken and quiet. They usually try hard to see the good in people and they tend to take pride in being pleasant to others. These children like things and people to stay just the way they are. They prefer to listen and may try to prove "just how nice they can be." These children may allow other children to get the attention or take the center stage. They do not have to be the star but they do like sincere recognition. These children are frequently commended on their report cards because of their ability to get along with other children and be part of a team. You can identify these children by how well they listen, by how well they cooperate with other children and by their relaxed easy-going energy.

BEHAVIORAL CATEGORY 4

CAUTIOUS AND CONCERNED ABOUT DOING THINGS CORRECTLY

Children with this behavioral style like to do things correctly. They like to plan ahead and know what the rules are. They prefer to know the exact answers. They may like their rooms organized and neat. They usually like to have time to think before deciding anything. They may sometimes fret and worry. They are probably very careful of key details, such as how they take care of their favorite toys. They may ask probing questions which seem too adult for them. You can identify these children by how carefully they do their tasks, by how well they follow the rules and by the nature of their questions, which may seem somewhat critical or probing.

As you read through the descriptions, it is very important not to judge or label children. There is no best behavioral style or category. Humans have natural behaviors which they use to get their needs met. This language describes those natural behaviors. Many people have a judgmental reaction to their own natural behavior. (They judge their own behavior as the best and the behavioral styles of others as wrong. They may reason: "Since we are different, those other behaviors must be wrong.") There is not one best behavioral style or way to act. There are different ways people use to get their needs met. Children need to be directed as to how to use their natural behaviors effectively and appropriately.

Remember, most children show all of the behaviors at some time, depending on the situation. For example, a Cautious child, when accused unjustly of making a mistake, might tell her mother: "Mother, I told you two days ago that I had to have the colored pencils for art class today." In this situation, the child's "telling" communication style appears to be more like the Active, Decisive child's behaviors. Yet, this telling behavior is not her most common or frequent behavior. Situationally, children and adults will use each of the four behaviors. The child's natural behavior is the one or two behavioral categories she uses most frequently and consistently. These one or two categories are the most comfortable behaviors for the child.

Please do not use this language to judge your children as wrong or "not O.K." As humans we do this enough already. Children often spend the first years of their lives listening to adults telling them how "wrong" they are and how they must be different to be loved or accepted. This is incredibly shaming. Often a child learns there is something innately wrong or bad about her.

This behavioral language is meant to offer you a new language for understanding and accepting your children. With this language you can communicate with your children and esteem their natural behavior while guiding them toward flexibility and adaptability. It is critically important to use this language to understand the natural differences that occur in human behavior. This language is a tool to nurture and honor the behaviors of your children and yourself.

3

Who are the Children

Children experience all types of emotions from anger to joy. Yet, within this range of emotions, each child has a basic disposition which reflects the self-concept of the child, including his genetic predisposition and his environmental influences. Understanding this disposition is the key to seeing the world from the child's point of view. When parents and teachers understand the child's point of view, they have insights into the behaviors which stem from it.

Children from Behavioral Category 1 have a basic disposition of independence and a strong sense of self. This sense of self may appear as a focus on their own activities or needs. This means the child's attention is often on "What I want!" Because these children are confident in self, or self-confident; they often dare to be different. They are naturally motivated to express their individualism by not relying on others and by pursuing their independent course of thought and action regardless of what the others think. They may stand out as different from other kids. They may express this individualism by developing unusual interests or ignoring certain rules which everyone else follows. Their self-confidence is often evident by their ability to take risks and their natural autonomy. This autonomy, or need to be free from outside control, may easily turn into a power struggle with parents and teachers. When their independence is threatened, these children often display irritation or anger.

The basic disposition of children from Behavioral Category 2 is focused toward accepting others. This means that these children tend to express general approval of others as opposed to forming a judgment about others. In fact, these children convey their acceptance of others with their verbal and nonverbal behaviors. Parents report that these children readily start conversations with almost everyone in the supermarket. This acceptance of others comes from the child's natural drive to be accepted. These children are naturally motivated to use a range of behaviors to interact with others so that they gain approval. Their sense of confidence and worth comes from the approval they gain. When they are unable to gain approval from a teacher or parent, they may feel an intense loss of self-worth which can lead to tears and disruptive behaviors.

The children from Behavioral Category 3 have an obliging or accommodating disposition. Obliging behavior means to secure needs by favors or services. Remember, everyone is motivated to get their needs met. Children from each of the behavioral categories use different behaviors to get their needs met. The Category 3 child secures his needs by using accommodating behaviors such as offering favors or service to others. Because these children are focused on obliging others, especially their parents and teachers, they will listen closely to what the adults in their lives say. These children are motivated to figure out how to be accommodating. They do this by watching what happens to others. If these children see someone getting in trouble for doing something wrong, they won't try the same unaccommodating behavior. In new situations, when they do not know what behaviors will be accommodating, they will ask questions and stay on the sidelines observing until they know what behaviors will oblige the others who are present. Most parents and teachers describe these children as "easy-to-handle-children" because they try hard not to cause any trouble or disruption. Even when they engage in natural conflicts with other children, they may try to quarrel quietly. In their attempt to be obliging, these children may even try not to be too demanding of parents and teachers.

The disposition of children from Behavioral Category 4 is focused on avoiding or rejecting the dominance or hostility of others. Because of their high need for peace and tranquillity, these children will often try "pleasing behaviors" to avoid arousing aggression in others. To get their needs met, these children will try hard to remember the rules at home and at school. By remembering the rules, they are often able to meet their need for safety from aggressive people. The rules often protect them from being aggressive themselves. Instead of being assertive, which might lead to a conflict, they will use "the rule" to assert their rights. In fact, they may remind their siblings or classmates of the rules with statements like:

"You're supposed to raise your hand before you talk." Another child may have said, "It was my turn, you interrupted me!"

"My mom won't let me eat my dessert until I've eaten my sandwich." Another child may have said, "I like peanut butter and jelly. I want to eat my sandwich first!"

"These shorts are supposed to go with the blue shirt." Another child may have said, "Everyone else gets to wear sweatshirts, I want to wear my blue one."

Although normally quiet and reserved, this child may have volumes to say if you ask: "Are there different rules at school than at home?" or "Which rules do the students in your class break the most frequently?"

The natural ways of behaving which individuals use to get their needs met are called their behavioral intentions or goals. A behavioral intention is simply what the individual has in mind or does to bring about meeting his needs. This means that each child is naturally motivated to behave in ways that allow him to reach his behavioral goals.

Children from Behavioral Category 1 have a behavioral goal of dominance and independence. In a child's life, dominance frequently means: being "the boss," being able to tell others what to do or being the one who has the authority. Teachers and parents may complain because these children frequently "do not do what they are told." When a parent or teacher says "don't do that" to a child who has dominance as a goal, it's as if the adult has drawn a line in the sand. The child may perceive the line in the sand as something to challenge or control. Most certainly, the child will want to determine the consequences for stepping over the line and will probably step over the line, or at least get as close as possible to the line, to see what happens. The double focus of dominance and independence means these children want to be free of controls, rules and restraints. They don't want to get permission. They don't want to ask someone to help them. Parents may frequently hear: "I want to do it by myself!" One of the largest challenges of teaching or parenting this child is that the child will frequently want control and independence in situations he has not developed the ability to handle, for example:

> Three and a half year old Karen, in her drive to assert her dominance and independence, said to her mother, "I want the top off my orange juice like Dad did." Her mother tried to convince Karen that leaving the foil top on the disposable juice container and using a straw would be better, since the plastic glass was so tippy and prone to spilling. She continued to appeal to Karen by showing how Laura did it. Six year old Laura had poked her straw through the foil. But Karen was determined to control the situation and demanded the foil top be removed. The foil top was removed and within seconds Karen spilled the juice. Juice soaked her clothes and she started to cry. As her mother held and comforted her, Karen cried, "Mom, **you** should have left the foil ..." and then she stopped and said in a small voice, "Oh, **I** should have left the foil on ..."

The most important element in this situation was that Karen was allowed to experience the consequences of her own behaviors. Yes, it was unpleasant for her to be sticky and soaked with juice. But it could have been just as unpleasant for Karen to wage an ongoing breakfast battle with her mother over control for her juice. If this had been a hot liquid which could have burned her, Karen's mother may have chosen to be more assertive. The key is for the adult to choose carefully the critical situations in which it would be dangerous to the child's safety if the child was allowed to be in control or independent.

Children from Behavioral Category 2 have a behavioral intention of gaining approval and popularity. These children are other-focused. Most importantly, they want others to like them. Because their intention is to gain the admiration and regard of others, these children will often have highly developed social skills. They will use a range of behaviors to get others to like them: smiling easily, asking others to play, spending time with others, giving gifts, offering compliments, accepting others' inappropriate behaviors and engaging in group activities to gain more contact with others. One of the biggest parental challenges is to help these children balance their need for gaining approval with their rights and responsibilities to their own work and themselves.

Security is the intention or behavioral goal of the children from Behavioral Category 3. These children usually want things to stay the way they are because they know they can cope with what is "known to them." Predictability is important, as it brings with it a security of knowing what is going to happen. Routines such as having pizza on Friday nights and always having one story before bedtime bring a sense of security to these children. Of course, a stable home life is important to all children. But, in the case of children from Category 3, a break in routine may create anxiety or alarm. Remember, these children have a natural drive to reach the goal of living in a consistent, predictable environment because it gives them the security they need. Parents and teachers of these children will need to help them learn to manage the natural disruptions in life; such as a late supper, no bedtime story, a new teacher, a new baby-sitter, a friend moving away and a sibling going to school. These children will need special guidance to learn how to accept the changes which naturally occur as they grow up.

The goal or behavioral intention of Category 4 children is to be correct. Correct in this context means to "conform to a standard or rule." Because these children need peace and tranquillity, they are motivated to behave according to the rules and avoid doing anything that would negatively effect their harmony. In particular, these children want to avoid making mistakes that might annoy others. For Cautious children, it is easier to be correct and follow the rules when they do not have to interact with others who don't know or care about the rules. Because of this, Cautious children often prefer to be alone and want private time. These children take great pains not only to learn the rules but to internalize them. The rules often become second nature. These children want their "special toys" in their proper place. They may be frustrated when their efforts at coloring or drawing do not meet their standards. Although they probably won't say it out loud or show it, these children may feel angry when a teacher messes up an immaculate paper with red marks or when a parent doesn't fold the bedspread back in a tidy manner. Parents and teachers will need to help these children develop a greater comfort with making mistakes. Although it is unlikely that these children will ever be totally comfortable with making mistakes, it will be critical that they develop the understanding that mistakes are often valuable tools in learning.

In order to further understand a child's world from his point of view, it is important to appreciate how children perceive the actions of others. Each child perceives other people's behaviors from his own needs. In addition, each child expresses his perceptions of others through his actions. This means children from each of the four behavioral categories have different reactions to the actions of other people.

The Active, Decisive child from Behavioral Category 1 forms an opinion of others based on their ability to quickly get things done. These children prefer to take action quickly and perceive that others should act quickly too. The mother of six year old Steve offers an explanation of how watchful she must be with her Active, Decisive child:

"One evening we were having dinner at a Chinese buffet with friends. Everyone was just starting to eat when I noticed Steve's chair was empty. He had already eaten his food and decided to go back for more. When I got up to find him, he was on tiptoe trying to reach over his head into the buffet steam tray to spear egg rolls. When I took his plate to help him, he said, 'You're so slow Mother; I would have already gotten three egg rolls by now.'"

These children may be so concerned with "speedily getting the task done" that they don't pay attention to the details. In the classroom, they may start the assignment before they understand the directions. They will be the ones who are most annoyed with a teacher who takes too long to explain the assignment. In addition, they may be very impatient with other children who do not move as quickly as they do. A common complaint from these children may be "I don't want to be on his team. He doesn't get it done fast enough." Both parents and teachers can affirm these children's wonderful, quick energy while guiding them toward understanding the importance of slow, thoughtful energy by saying things like:

"Your quick energy is wonderful and in some situations you will want to choose to do things slower."

"Can you think of times when moving slower would work more effectively?"

"You're good at doing things fast. Can you be as good at doing _____ (task) slowly?"

Interactive children from Behavioral Category 2 may perceive that quieter, reserved people don't like them. These children are usually bubbly, optimistic and excitable. From their point of view, other people are in the world so they can talk to them. Someone who doesn't talk with them must not like them.

In school, these children may be stunned when they first meet a teacher who is reserved and uses words sparingly. James is a good example of this. After his first day in the new third grade class, James told his mother: "Mr. Blake doesn't like me! I'm never going back to school!"

After much talking, James' mother learned that he based this perception on the fact that Mr. Blake rarely smiled and didn't say much during recess. James' mother explained that Mr. Blake was more reserved than his previous teacher and he would show his emotions in quieter ways.

James perceived that Mr. Blake's nonverbals were messages about James. This is a common perception of Category 2 children. They interpret the nonverbals, talkativeness or lack of interaction, as a personal message about how much someone likes or dislikes them. The teachers and parents of these children need to explain: "Other people have different ways of interacting and it is important not to assume that people are sending messages about us, simply because they act differently." These children need to learn that others may not talk or share information the way they do. They need to be guided toward understanding that other people have different ways of behaving toward people. A parent or teacher may say:

"You consider friends very important and you would like almost everyone to be your friend. Sometimes there may be people who don't want to be friends. It isn't possible to have everyone like you all the time. Because someone isn't your friend, it doesn't mean you are not O.K. It does say something about the other person. Some children want only one or two friends. Other children may take a long time before they build a friendship with you. Some children may want to compete with you. If someone is not friendly toward you, it doesn't mean that you've done something wrong."

The children from Behavioral Category 3, Soft-spoken and Cooperative, perceive the people in their world according to their friendships. They are usually mild-mannered in their interactions with others. Like the Talkative, Animated children, friends are important to them, but they are not focused on "everyone" the way the interactive children are. Instead, Category 3 children usually have a small group of close friends. They tend to be naturally tolerant of others. They usually tolerate others' mistakes and may try to explain the mistakes in the most favorable way. With friends they are even more tolerant, often overlooking inappropriate behaviors with statements like: "Oh, Kathy's just like that; she doesn't mean anything by it." Because these children often perceive others' behaviors through a filter of kindness, they filter out many of the negative behaviors. They tend to focus on those behaviors which support their view that others are really being kind; they are just misinterpreted or making honest mistakes. The challenge for parents and teachers of these children is to help them develop a more realistic view of others. Although we would like to believe that all people have our best interests at heart, some people are not kind and trustworthy. It is critical for these children to gain an objective view of others and the skills for handling inappropriate behaviors.

The Cautious children from Behavioral Category 4 form opinions of others based on what others know and how they use what they know. Remember, it is the behavioral intention of these children to live correctly, according to the rules, in order to gain peace and tranquillity in their lives. So it makes sense that these children prefer people who are thoughtful and who will guide them in taking the correct actions. These children may spend considerable time thinking about "what is the right thing to do or say." Although these children will rarely overtly reject anyone, they will choose friends who think before they act and who know how to behave according to the rules of the situation. For example, Cautious children know there are different rules for how to behave in school, at home, at a soccer game, at a picnic and with adults. They will prefer friends who know the rules and follow them. When their friends do not follow the rules, they may be so frustrated that they are driven to tears, as Laura was in the following illustration:

> Seven year old Laura and her friend Patty were huddled together playing in the "Fort," a table draped with blankets, when Patty stopped playing "Fort" and quietly began bouncing a ball. Laura explained, "Patty, bouncing the ball isn't playing Fort." Patty ignored Laura and continued playing with the ball.

> By the time Laura's mother arrived, Laura was close to tears. Patty wouldn't play "Fort" by the rules and she wouldn't leave the Fort. Laura's frustration was increased by the fact that Patty, her friend, didn't understand her explanations or the innate rules which went with playing Fort. Laura was not only frustrated with the lack of attention to the rules, but she was dismayed to discover that her friend didn't "think" the same way she did. Although Laura did not say anything to Patty about the incident, Laura silently stored the following information: "Patty can't understand some of the rules, so when I play with her I'll play simpler games, but I don't think I'll play "Fort" with her again."

Parents and teachers need to affirm the discernment which Cautious children have, while encouraging them to focus on a balanced understanding of others. Laura's mother could say to her:

> "Patty doesn't always understand your rules and I'm glad that you have the ability to see that. Sometimes people don't have the qualities we want to see in them. It's also important to see the positive qualities that people do have. Patty has some things that you like about her. What are some of the things you like to do with Patty? Can you try to do more of the things you like to do with Patty when she comes over to play?"

Each of the children from the four behavioral categories has unique ways of associating with others. Teachers may talk about how well a child socializes with his peers. Parents often focus on how the child "gets along" with siblings, friends and teachers. But children are usually not aware there are different ways to "get along." From their limited experiences and even more limited self-awareness, children often have no comprehension of how others are affected by their behaviors. Yet, every teacher and parent knows the affect a child's behavior can have on any situation. A simple grocery shopping trip can turn into an exhausting experience with an angry two year old. A class outing can be an ongoing power struggle for a determined teenager. A drive in the car can turn into a sibling battle over who sat by the window last time. It is important for parents and teachers to understand how children are naturally motivated to treat others.

Children from Behavioral Category 1 are forceful and direct with others. When they want something from another person they will strive to get it. Parents gave the following examples of their Active, Decisive child's directness:

When his mother bought turkey instead of bologna for lunch, three year old Alex rolled on the floor of the Deli and screamed.

When ten year old Carla wasn't chosen as a room monitor, she asked her teacher every morning if it was her turn yet.

At the park, seven year old Jim was invited to play with his eleven year old brother and his brother's older friends. Jim insisted that they play basketball but everyone voted for baseball. Jim was so outraged that his brother had to walk him home so his mother could calm him down.

The home team was winning when thirteen year old Kevin was benched so that a less-able player could play. Kevin tried to talk his coach into changing his decision. When that didn't work, he spiked the ball and drew a penalty.

Regardless of their age, these children are not easily discouraged. With their strong sense of self, they do not think twice about "telling" others what they should do. They do not hesitate to demand their rights. Because they often struggle for

control of their environment, parents and teachers have to focus on:
- helping them develop negotiation skills,
- when their force and persistence is a strength and
- how to deal with the terrible pain they feel when their desires are thwarted.

Parents and teachers will have to be especially careful about staying out of power struggles with these children. In any power struggle these children have a large chance of winning.

The children from Behavioral Category 2 are naturally motivated to give compliments and approval to others. These children focus on others. They want others to like them so badly that they may become primarily "givers." Parents may not see this giving behavior as strongly at home, since being liked and loved at home is more secure then being liked at school. Teachers may comment about the verbal and social skills these children demonstrate. Because these children have an incredible willingness to share their feelings and an ability to "read" others, they frequently are the barometers for the class, as in the following situations:

When six year old Sara says, "I think the lunch room is scary because we have to eat with all the sixth and seventh-graders," a teacher can surmise that many of the other first graders are scared at lunch.

When fourteen year old Matt says, "Coach, I think everybody feels bad because we didn't win," the coach can assume that most of the team would like the coach to reassure them about their athletic worthiness.

When ten year old Alicia pleads, "Mom, please don't yell at dad. It makes my stomach hurt," her mother can presume that her outburst has frightened all the kids.

Because these children are motivated to get others to like them, they are often seen as nice, social and needing little guidance with others. It is important that these children learn discernment skills about the motives of others so they are not taken advantage of, for example:

Sue wanted others to like her so much that she frequently did their homework for them.

Pete wanted to be popular so badly that he used his allowance to buy candy for others.

Sam was very hurt when he loaned his mountain bike to a "friend" who lost it.

When guiding these children who desire acceptance and approval, parents need to continually explain:

"Giving to others is wonderful AND it is important to give to yourself sometimes."

"Talking with others is important and sometimes it is important to listen."

"Wanting to be liked is O.K. Sometimes you may not be liked and you are still a good person."

The Soft-spoken and Cooperative children are motivated to accommodate others and to be consistent. They have an ability to cooperate with others so they can play together. These children innately know how to get along with others. Because they are motivated to cooperate with others, they are often the grease that allows the different parts of a group to work together. As part of their ability to accommodate, these children appear to have a wide range of responses to different types of people: with Active, Decisive children they will usually submit, with Talkative children they will often listen and with Cautious children they will be encouraging. Children who need to talk to someone will seek out these children because of their ability to listen. While the Category 2 child's talkative, social nature is hard to miss, the Category 3 child is often reserved and quiet. The Soft-spoken, Cooperative child will be accommodating to all types of individuals and he will select a limited number of close friends for special treatment. This special treatment may include supporting his friends in trouble and celebrating with his friends who are successful. Because of his low-key behavior, it may be hard to observe the range of accommodating behaviors he uses with his peer group and friends. What is easier to see is the child's consistent behavior concerning his chores. These children usually brush their teeth before bedtime, wash their hands before meals, finish their homework before watching TV and generally behave day in and day out in a uniform manner. Many parents and teachers compliment themselves for raising "well-behaved-children," when in actuality their behaviors are naturally self-motivated.

Cautious children are most often curious and factual with others. They usually have a wealth of stored knowledge which may surprise the adults. For example:

Four year old Alan was eating lunch with his mother, father, aunt and uncle. As they were eating lunch his Aunt Joan asked, "What is your favorite toy?"

"My dinosaur," he responded and then asked, "Do you know how to spell dinosaur?"

Joan replied, "D i n a s a u r."

"No," he said calmly, "it's spelled D i n o s a u r."

"I don't think you're right," interjected his mother. "Let's get the dictionary and see what the correct spelling is."

Needless to say everyone was surprised when four year old Alan was the only one to spell dinosaur correctly. The amount of information which these children have is hardly surprising when you consider that they are naturally motivated to gather the "facts." Books are often just as important as friends to these children who like to gain knowledge in whatever form they can. In fact, they will frequently quote adults:

"My Dad says, you should never wrap the cord around a power tool because you can damage the cord."

"The teacher says you should eat fruit everyday."

"My Mother says you lose heat through your head, so if it's cold outside and you want to stay warm, you should wear a hat."

Although all children have questions about their world, Cautious children's natural persistence for more and more information may be irritating. Common examples of these children's probing questions are:

"Mrs. Blaine, you said that God created the world, right? Well, if God created the world, who created God?"

"Dad, why do the electrical plug-ins have only two prongs?"

"Mommy, who decided that school starts at 8:15. Why not 8:16?"

"Why doesn't grampa wear a seatbelt? The
television said that everyone should wear a seatbelt."
"Why are there different colors of people? Why are
some people born with birth defects? Why does it rain?"
"But you said that the sun always come up in the
morning. Why does it come up at different times?"

These children use their powers of observation to ask
questions about their environment. They will have questions
about people, nature, times, spaces and much more. They use
this information to explain and examine their world. If they have
carefully examined their world and can understand it, then they
can live "correctly," which is their behavioral intent. Although
their questions can often steer others to the correct answers,
these children need to be cautioned about how others may
perceive their questions. Teachers may think these children are
troublemakers because they ask questions which sidetrack the
class work. The children may be perceived by their parents as
trying to stump them or show up their lapses in knowledge.
Others may perceive the questions as hidden criticisms. For the
most part, these children have no awareness their thirst for
knowledge could upset anyone.

By developing a deeper understanding of a child's
behavioral disposition, intentions, perceptions of others and
ways of associating with others, adults have the unique
opportunity to see the world from the child's point of view.
These children's unique perceptions offer us the framework to
develop teaching and parenting strategies which can guide and
direct the children to more effective ways of behaving.

4

Active, Decisive Children

Betty had two boys, Sam and Kurt, ages two and four. Her friend and next door neighbor, Janet, was the mother of Keith and John, ages four and six. When Betty was chasing Sam down the street or trying to manage his Active, Decisive behavior, Janet would shake her head and say, "Betty, you just have to discipline Sam. Look at my two boys. They don't cause me a bit of trouble. Consistent discipline is the key." Betty would retort, "I do discipline him. He still has a mind of his own."

Janet continually tried to help Betty improve her parenting skills by giving her books and suggestions for handling Sam. When Sam was three, Janet gave birth to Jeremy. When Sam was five, Janet was chasing Jeremy down the street. When Sam was six, Janet admitted, "I used to think it was discipline. I used to think that you were doing something wrong because Sam was out of control so often, but Jeremy is just like him. It was so easy with my other two children. Jeremy is twice the handful they were at this age. I'm sorry I blamed you for not being enough of a parent."

Parents of Active and Decisive (Category 1) children frequently wonder: "What am I doing wrong?" They may look at other children who are more easy-going and obedient and feel guilty or blame themselves for not "figuring out how to be a better parent." Or, they may blame the child and believe that the child is somehow flawed. Parents of Active, Decisive children often have the most interesting stories to tell, for example:

Danny's mother says, "From the beginning of his life Danny was determined to do exactly what he wanted to do. When he was eight months old, Danny would grab my eyeglasses and scream for several minutes when they were taken away. He would not be consoled. I tried distracting techniques, which worked with my other children, such as giving him his favorite toy or a cookie. I was desperate to get his attention away from my glasses. Nothing worked. Danny would not be distracted; he would protest loudly with great bellowing and loud crying when he was thwarted. I tried everything; I held his squirming body; I got him a pair of old glasses to play with; I tried to ignore his demanding crying; I tried consoling him; I tried everything. It didn't matter what I did. Danny would yell for several minutes before he was ready to resume his playing. I even had an elderly neighbor who came over to check on Danny to see if I was abusing him. It was embarrassing. But all she found was Danny sitting on the floor, surrounded by toys, howling."

Jessica's Mother tells this experience. "When Jessica was a year old, she would reach for a forbidden object and look at me to see if I was watching. I would say 'No! No! Jessica.' She would smile and reach for the object. When I removed the object, Jessica would yell with frustration. Of course, I quickly learned to put away any forbidden objects. But Jessica was often able to find something she shouldn't have. She was as fast as the speed of light. She could find a cord from a lamp and be playing with the electrical socket before I could blink. We had to remove several lamps and plug all the sockets with child protection caps."

Karen's father tells of his experience. "When Karen was two years old, she was brushing her teeth at the sink next to her older sister. Karen wanted the sink, so she pushed her older sister aside. Laura, who was six, ignored the push and kept brushing her teeth. Karen turned and bit Laura's arm, refusing to let go even when I picked her up and said 'NO! STOP BITING!' Finally, in desperation, I thumped Karen on the head with my finger and she let go."

The summer when Seth was two and a half he learned how to open the gate at the end of his yard. Even though he'd been warned and disciplined about slipping out through the gate, his mother did not dare take her eyes off him when he was outside. All she had to do was talk to another child or turn her back for a second and Seth would make a dash for the gate. The frightening part was that in less than two seconds Seth could be out in the street. Through incredible watchfulness, a new gate lock which took longer to open and many "time outs" for Seth; Seth and his mother made it through the summer.

By the time Jimmy was three, he'd been trying to tell his mother what to do for almost a year. As Jimmy's verbal skills grew, each day often brought a new power struggle. Jimmy, strapped in his car seat, told his mother where to park the car. When his mother thanked him for his attention but parked closer to the building, Jimmy started yelling and would not stop. After sitting in the car for five minutes with Jimmy's hollering, his mother drove home without getting out of the car. Jimmy continued hollering for the entire drive home.

Three and a half year old Cindy was having breakfast with her father. Cindy chose her cereal, wheat flakes, and told her father, "You have the corn flakes." Cindy's father poured granola into his cereal bowl. Cindy tried for the next five minutes to coerce her father into having a different cereal. First she got the box of corn flakes and put it on the table next to her father. Then she slid the box into her father's cereal bowl. When her father put the box of corn flakes away, Cindy went to the cupboard and got it out again. Before breakfast was over, Cindy's father finally agreed to have a few corn flakes in his bowl of granola, just so that he could eat breakfast in peace.

Lila's mother offers these examples about what life was like with her Active, Decisive twelve year old daughter. "I knew I had to learn some new parenting skills to deal with this child as almost every meal, every decision, every new pair of jeans was rapidly becoming a power struggle. So I enrolled in a college course on behavior modification. It was so simple. I was just to sit down and talk with Lila about what I wanted and allow her input into the goal. After she achieved the goal, I would reward her behavior. I started with cleaning her room. After some discussion, Lila and I agreed she would be rewarded with extra privileges for each week in which her room was clean. She would lose privileges when her room was not clean. After the first successful week I knew I had the answer. But the second week Lila's room returned to the disheveled mess of dirty clothes, papers and books scattered around and leftover food molding on her night stand, so I told her she had lost some of her privileges. The third week the mess in the room continued and I informed Lila that she'd lost a few more privileges. By the fourth week, Lila took me aside and said, 'Mother, you might as well give it up; I don't care how many privileges you take away. There is NOTHING you can do to make me clean up my room if I don't want to!' 'But, Lila,' I responded, 'it worked so well the first week.' 'That's only because I wanted it to, and now I don't,' stated Lila. After that I handled the power struggles on a situation to situation basis. I made sure that I only engaged when it was of the utmost importance, otherwise Lila would have been fighting with me all the time. The one thing that I was not able to get her to do was take a bath. She was absolutely dirty most of the time she was twelve and thirteen. No amount of persuasion, coercion, threats, pleading, negotiating, or rewards would tempt Lila to take a bath. I finally gave up. Sometime around her sixteenth birthday she started a more regular bathing routine, but she started bathing because she was getting messages from her boyfriend that she smelled! Believe it or not, Lila went to college, got her masters degree in business and is a very successful business woman in Atlanta. But, there were times I didn't think we'd make it through the week."

Stuart's father relates his experience, "I enjoyed being in a fraternity when I was in college. I thought Stuart would enjoy it too. So, one afternoon I initiated a discussion about the pros and cons of fraternities. Eighteen year old Stuart said, 'Dad, you don't understand. You have greater needs for people than I do. You really care what people think. I don't.' "

Many childhood developmental studies discuss the ages most children will test their independence and autonomy. Most parents and teachers are aware that all children will test the rules once in a while. They are aware of the determination a small child can display in a toy store when she finds the toy she wants. It is common for all children to test their independence and autonomy by pushing against their parent's authority. But, the children from Category 1 (Active and Decisive) are naturally motivated toward independence and autonomy at all stages of life. When they are in the common childhood stages of developing independence, such as during the teenage years, their natural drive toward independence and autonomy often becomes even more intense.

Parents who raise Active, Decisive children admit to moments of panic when they think, "I don't think I'm up to the challenge of raising this kid!" Yet, these same parents speak with pride of their successful adult children. Parents are brutally honest when they say: "My Active, Decisive child was a handful to raise. I learned a lot about myself in the process, and it was worth it."

If you are the parent or teacher of Active, Decisive children, it is vital that you have a planned, well-thought-out strategy for guiding these children. If you haven't figured out how to respond before you get to a conflict, these children will be able to pull you into a power struggle the majority of the time. Each time they win a power struggle, you have reinforced their tendency to use power struggles to get what they want. Even if they don't have a chance to win, they will have an opportunity to test themselves against you – a natural challenge they will usually welcome.

To develop a well-thought-out strategy for interacting with an Active, Decisive child, it is important to consider: the natural behavior of the child, how to identify and manage power plays and an understanding of what are caring, esteeming consequences for inappropriate behaviors.

The natural behavior of the Active, Decisive child is to "control her world." Therefore, it is critical that the child have control of areas in her life which are appropriate to her age and readiness level. Power and control come from the ability to choose. These children need guidance to determine how to exercise their control through their choices. As a parent or teacher, it is critical to determine which areas are in the child's control and which areas are not negotiable. It may be helpful to list the areas in which the child can exercise her control.

Although each child has a different readiness level based on the child's abilities, a sample list of choices can be helpful when creating your list of choices for the first time.

A SAMPLE, PARTIAL LIST for the parents of a three year old could include these areas of choice:

CLOTHES – the child may choose from two or three offered outfits. The child is not in charge of the following non-negotiable areas:

1. clothing inappropriate for the situation, such as an expensive velvet dress in which to play outdoors,

2. clothing related to weather, such as whether or not to wear a coat when it is freezing outside,

3. clothing inappropriate for the safety of the child, such as a Halloween mask which obstructs the child's vision.

FOOD – the child may choose from an offered selection of food, such as: a choice of which fruit – an apple, a banana or a pear, or a choice of a peanut butter sandwich or a cheese sandwich. If the child chooses not to make a choice from the offered items, she may choose not to eat. The non-negotiable may involve sugary foods such as candy, soft drinks and desserts which may not be eaten in place of breakfast, lunch or dinner.

NAP TIME – the child may choose one book and one toy to play with while she rests. It is not negotiable whether or not the child has a rest period. What is the child's choice is whether she naps or plays quietly with the toys she has chosen.

The following dialogue may offer a glimpse into the patience and constancy a parent or teacher must have to interact with an Active, Decisive child who is determined to control her world. The first dialogue frequently occurs when young children try to pull a parent into a power struggle.

Parent
"Would you like to wear the blue sweater or the red one?"

Child
"I want to wear my velvet dress."

Parent
Ignoring the response, "Which shoes would you like to wear, your tennis shoes or your sandals?"

Child
> "I want to wear my velvet dress."

Parent
> Maintaining a level voice, "Would you like to wear the blue sweater or the red one?"

Child
> Getting much louder, "I want to wear my velvet dress."

Parent
> "If you can't choose between the red sweater and the blue one, then I'll have to choose. Let's see which sweater would be best for you today. I think you should wear the ... the ... the ... red one."

Child
> "NO! NO! I want the velvet dress!!"

Parent
> Matter-of-factly, "The velvet dress is not a choice. If you don't make your choices this morning, I will get to pick. Let's see, I think you should wear the red sweater."

Child
> "NO! I want the blue one."

Parent
> Going on to the next choice, "Do you want to put it on by yourself or do you want help?"

As you can see from the dialogue, the parent is calmly repeating the child's choices. When the child tries to take control, the parent starts to make the child's choices for her. This is a loss of control for the child. The parent willingly capitulates to the child's demand for her rightful areas of control, which the parent previously identified as belonging to the child.

Many a morning has dissolved into a power struggle with a young Active, Decisive child. The parent can resist being pulled into power struggles by continuing to repeat the child's choices. If the situation continues to escalate, which is not uncommon, the parent can withdraw the choices which are rightfully the child's, thereby demonstrating to the child that her behavior causes her to forfeit her limited power of choice.

If the parent gives in and the child wears the velvet dress, the parent has sent the message that the child has control about which clothes she will wear and she will fight even harder tomorrow so that she maintains control.

It is critical that parents be able to maintain their focus about "which decision" the child gets to make. Often, Active, Decisive children are very capable of redirecting the parent's attention to their agenda. The following dialogue is a good example of this redirecting ability:

Parent
"Which book do you want to take with you for your nap?"

Child
"I don't want to nap."

Parent
"Which toy do you want? I think you should take your doll, Rosy."

Child
"I don't want to nap. I won't nap."

Parent
Trying to be persuasive, "Now Honey, if you don't nap you'll be tired when we go out to dinner tonight with Uncle Jim and Aunt Alice."

Child
"I won't nap. I'm a big boy. I don't need a nap. I won't do it."

Parent
"Yes, you will!"

Child
"NO, I WON'T!"

Parent
With anger, "YES, YOU WILL!"

Child
Yelling loudly, "NO! NO! NO!"

Parent
Yelling loudly, "YES! YES! YES!"

In this dialogue, the child was able to pull the parent into a shouting match, thus proving his ability to control his environment by creating a power struggle and delaying the much dreaded nap. A real sense of his power to control his environment is evident in his ability to "control his parent's emotions." He was, after all, able to get his parent angry and shouting.

The parents must know the areas of control which they will not capitulate to the child. These areas must not be open to negotiation. In the first dialogue, the parents have agreed that the child is not at the readiness level to generally choose the clothes she will wear, as she is unable to dress for the situation (i.e., the velvet dress is not appropriate for playing outdoors).

In the second dialogue, the non-negotiable should be that the child is not able to control whether or not he takes a rest period. He can, however, control whether he sleeps or what books he reads. He can also control the nap time by yelling for the entire period, but he does not get to decide whether or not he has a "rest time."

If the parent is consistent with the choices offered, the child will spend less time pushing for greater choices. However, if the parent allows the child to wear the velvet dress, eat candy for lunch or not take a nap because of a tantrum, the child will receive reinforcement about her ability to control and she will be driven to do what she needs to do to maintain her control.

One important caution for parents and teachers. Because these children are naturally motivated to control their world, they may want to control you. A common response to a child who wants to control a parent or teacher is for the adult to overpower the child. They child's reaction is to protest with sentences like, "No, you can't make me do that." When these familiar situations occur, the adult frequently judges the child as "bad." These children are often labeled as "brats" or "troublemakers." The reality is that they are just children doing what comes naturally to them. They are not brats or troublemakers, they are simply trying, in their own inept, childish way, to get their natural needs met. They have not learned to cooperate or use different behaviors yet and they need firm guidance, not labels and judgments. Remember, these children may equate loss of control with loss of self! They may perceive themselves to be fighting for their very souls.

One excellent way of helping these children understand what their choices are and what their choices are not, is to have a book listing their choices. Parents and teachers can list the child's choices in the left hand column and the adult's choices in the right hand column. This may be too advanced for young children, but stickers and pictures of clothes or toys in the book will remind children of where they have control in their world. It also reminds the parent to be consistent. If a parent forgets whose choice it is or sees a power struggle developing, getting down "the choice book" and checking who gets to choose can be a handy way of defusing the conflict. As the child grows, the parent can add the child's new choices, so the child can actually see her control of her world expanding.

In addition to identifying which choices belong to the child and which choices belong to the adult, it is important for the adults to develop skills for extracting themselves from power plays. The first step in understanding power plays with Active, Decisive children is to accept that the power plays are real. Then take an inventory of where these power plays most frequently occur. For example, a child may try power plays in stores and around other people if she senses parents are liable to give in because others are watching. Parents can learn to identify their own negative responses which can intensify the situation: responses such as embarrassment when others may not think you are a "good parent" or anger when the child continues to persist even when you have said "NO!" It is also important for parents and teachers to examine their personal beliefs which support power plays; beliefs such as:

- "If I were a good teacher, I wouldn't have trouble with this child."
- "A child who doesn't do what he is told is bad."
- "Children should obey their elders."
- "I would have never raised my voice to my father, my son should be the same."
- "Children should be seen and not heard."
- "Good children never cause any trouble."
- "Children should always have a hearty lunch even when they don't want to eat."

To deal effectively with power plays, both teachers and parents must learn compassionate detachment. Compassion in this context means that you are aware of how much you really do love this child. You may not love the child's behavior at the moment, but you do love the child. Detachment is the ability to separate yourself from both your beliefs and the situation, with the realization that the child is just trying to control her world. Detachment means not taking the child's behavior personally. Instead of engaging the child at her level in the power struggle, adults can detach and be still. With young children, adults may have to physically remove them from the situation before taking these steps. The important thing is for the parents to allow themselves all the time they need to maintain their detachment.

To detach, a parent may have to simply sit and look at the child without trying to get the child to do anything. When parents don't engage in the fight, they may be surprised to find their child intently watching them to determine "why they aren't getting angry or doing something." Once they've detached from the power struggle, parents can consider the child's choices, their choices and the consequences for the child's inappropriate behaviors. For example, instead of arguing with a child over whether or not he has candy for lunch, simply state the choices: "You can choose a peanut butter and jelly sandwich or a tuna fish sandwich." Then state the consequences, "You may have either of the sandwiches or you may choose not to eat."

Many parents will gasp with horror at the thought of their beloved child going hungry and the child knows that. The child can use her parent's fear of a hungry child to maintain power over the parent at meals.

When the child's choices have been identified and the parents or teachers have developed skills for extracting themselves from power struggles, it's time to develop long range strategies for guiding and nurturing these unique, special children.

The first step of a successful strategy involves the behavior of the parents and teachers. Whenever possible, avoid the following behaviors:
 • Telling the Active, Decisive child what to do.
 Example: "Jessica, pick up your toys, now!"
 • Criticizing or scolding the child, not the behavior.

Example: "You're a brat. You are terrible. You don't listen. You always want to fight. You want to cause trouble."
• Engaging in win-lose power struggles.
Example: "You will eat that peanut butter sandwich."

Whenever possible, parents and teachers can create more positive interactions with the Active, Decisive child by using a strategy of choices and consequences. Instead of telling the child what to do, offer choices.

> Example: "Do you want to pick up your toys before or after lunch?"

Instead of criticizing the child, reprimand the behavior and give consequences.

> Example: "It's not O.K.. to throw toys. You have a time out. Your behavior of _____(fill in the behavior) is not acceptable. This is what will happen _____(fill in the consequences)."

Instead of engaging in win-lose power struggles, whenever possible, emotionally detach from the anger or the intensity of the situation. Then repeat the child's choices and explain calmly the consequences of not choosing. If the situation escalates, remove the child or yourself.

> Example: "You may choose to buy the truck or the game. If you don't choose, we will leave immediately and you will not get either of them."

It is necessary to remain compassionate and yet detached from the emotional intensity of the power struggle, because any anger or intense emotion from the parent can focus the child's attention away from her behavior and toward the parent. One mother revealed how she learned about the importance of detachment during power struggles.

> "When my daughter was fourteen, almost everything became a power struggle until she inadvertently explained to me how I played a major role in each conflict. During this time, we were struggling financially and there were times we were short of money for food. One hot summer afternoon when I came home from work, I found the milk, mayonnaise and a breast of turkey on the counter by the kitchen sink. My daughter

was sitting at the kitchen table. I was tired of fighting with her. Instead, I calmly asked,

'How long has this food been out of the refrigerator?'

She answered flippantly, 'Since lunch.'

Without raising my voice I said, 'Please throw it all in the garbage, it's spoiled.'

Then without saying another word I walked out of the kitchen and went to my room to change my clothes. When I returned to the kitchen a few minutes later, I found my daughter with her arms held tightly at her sides. Her hands were in fists; tears streamed down her face.

'What's wrong?' I asked.

She cried, 'Please, Mother, get angry with me. If you'd only yell at me then I could be mad at you instead of being mad at myself!' "

The second part of a long range strategy with Active, Decisive children is to use communications which match their needs. These children prefer communications which are direct and to the point. Because of their intense involvement with "doing something," they may not hear you. You may have to touch them or talk in close proximity to gain their attention. They want to know "what we're going to do." They don't like extra talking. They prefer that you get to the point. Tell them the results they must achieve and what will happen when they get the results. AND, whenever possible, let them be in control of something in their world.

In the following example, the teacher allowed the child to control the worksheet. Since the student didn't have to wait for others who were slower, she could finish the worksheet quickly, find out the results or how many she did correctly and then get drawing paper. All these behaviors were under her control.

Example: Teacher speaking to her class, "Today we're going to talk about fractions. I will spend a few minutes explaining how to add fractions. Then, I will hand out a worksheet for you to do. By the end of math period, I will expect you to complete the fractions and check them with the answer key. When you've completed this, you can get drawing paper."

The third step in developing a successful strategy involves guiding the Active, Decisive child. These children need ongoing guidance in the areas of: competition, pace, intensity, active energy, boredom, negotiations, people, empathy, participation and patience.

Because these children have a natural motivation to dominate or control, competition brings out their drive to win. This is a very positive trait in situations such as a swimming meet or taking a test. However, the Active, Decisive child needs guidance from parents and teachers as to what situations are NOT competitive. Without this guidance, the child may perceive common situations as opportunities to win. Building a tree house with friends might turn into a competition to see who gets to be in charge. Sharing a piece of cake might turn into a competition to see who gets the biggest piece. Talking with the family could turn into a challenge to talk more than your sister.

It is important to guide these children toward cooperation while honoring their natural behaviors. A gym teacher could say: "Sometimes it's fun to see who is first, but today we're going to reward those children who cross the finish line together." A father coaching his daughter might say: "I know when you play with your friends you like to be the leader, but sometimes it's important that you choose to be a follower so that you learn to trust the leadership of other people."

The areas of pace and intensity are related to the child's need for dominance and independence. These children are naturally fast at getting things done. One of the ways they may judge the success of their work is how fast it was completed. In addition, they may increase their pace to maintain their "first done" status. They may be so intense about getting the task done that they become extremely serious. Humor can be an excellent way of lowering their intensity and redirecting their tight focus on getting the job done.

"Active energy" is often how parents initially describe their child's most natural behavior. This is not to say that all children don't have times of active energy, but the Active,

Decisive child has these behaviors much more frequently. In fact, the Active, Decisive child would like to be active all the time. Common questions asked by these children are "What shall we do next?" or "What's next?" or "When we finish this, what shall we do?" To guide this child toward developing a range of effective behaviors, both parents and teachers need to say things like:

"I like your active energy AND sometimes it's important to be quiet."

"We just had an active time playing outside, so now it is time for you to take a deep breath and see how many sounds you can hear."

"It is important to have lots of activity and it is just as important to have times of quiet and rest."

As a parent of young children, it is critical to have a schedule which allows the child plenty of large muscle activity first, before scheduling a quiet, restful story time. For the most part, these children will find it very hard to be still until they have had an opportunity to burn off some of their natural active energy. By developing a schedule which allows these children time to use their large muscles before they are asked to be quiet, adults may be surprised to find how much more manageable these children can be.

An Active, Decisive child riding for a long distance in a car may find it boring and poke or taunt her sister to alleviate the boredom. Often these children would rather get in trouble than be bored, as being in trouble is usually preferable to boredom. These bright, quick children are bored by the pace of the classroom, long distance rides, waiting or a rainy day when they can't play outside. Both parents and teachers need to plan activities to engage these children. Mental games which stress creativity, paper games where they can compete against themselves or games they can create are all examples of how these children can start to develop the internal discipline to use their mental resources to alleviate their boredom.

Negotiation skills are important for all children, but even more important for the Active, Decisive child. If the child can explain "what she wants and why she wants it," she can gather more information about how to behave effectively in a range of situations. For example, an Active, Decisive child is told by her father that she cannot ride her bike to the park because the brakes are faulty. So she walks to the park without telling anyone where she is going. When she gets home, her parents are furious that she disobeyed. Her parents could appreciate her point of view if she had the negotiation skills to say: "I thought I could go to the park. I thought you meant that I couldn't ride my bike there, not that I couldn't go! Anyway, why are you so upset, I knew where I was."

With an understanding of her point of view, the parents realize she didn't deliberately disobey them. They can respond, "I think there was a misunderstanding about the park. Even so, it is not enough that you know where you are, one of us must know where you are!"

Parents and teachers must take time to listen to these children. They have reasons for their behaviors which are often hard for them to explain. Because they like to do things quickly, they may respond "I don't know," when asked to explain their actions. Parents and teachers must remain calm and interested and ask gently, "Please explain to me what happened. I want to know. I know you had a good reason for doing what you did. Will you tell me?" Remember, these children do not deal well with any type of personal criticism, so parents and teachers will have to be prepared to say something like:
> "I know you had good intentions and you wanted
> things to turn out well. When something like this
> happens again, the behavior which will work better is
> _____ (fill in the blank)."

Because these children have such a strong sense of self, parents and teachers may neglect to esteem them for their natural behaviors. Remember, all children need to know they are loved, they are O.K., they are special, they do some things well and that it's O.K. to be who they are.

People, empathy and participation all have to do with coaching the Active, Decisive child's interactions with others. It is important to guide these children to an awareness of the needs of others. When the Active child always wants to be first in line, ask her, gently, how she feels when she has to be last in line Then explain that other children feel this way also, which is why it is important to let others be first sometimes. By helping the Active, Decisive child understand her feelings and needs, and then showing her that other people have feelings and needs also, the child can develop an understanding of her own motivations and more empathy for the feelings and needs of others. Patience is what the Active, Decisive child will need to learn to interact with others. Others will not usually move fast enough for her. She will sense that others will slow her down. In order to participate in groups or in classes, she will need to be coached on what patience is. A parent might say: "When you are at school, other children may not understand the information as quickly as you do. This may make you feel like you want to push them to get them to keep up with your fast pace. But, pushing others just makes them dislike you. It is better to take a deep breath and say to yourself 'I like to go fast, they go slower, and it's O.K. to be either fast or slow,' or 'When I am in a group I may have to slow down, but I can go as fast as I like when I'm working alone.' "

It is unrealistic for parents and teachers to expect these children to always participate. The Active, Decisive child who is forced to participate at school, during team sports and at home is likely to mutiny. These children need time for their individual interests. When they are alone they are in charge, so they can operate as fast as they want to get things done. This satisfies the Active, Decisive child's natural behavioral needs.

The Active, Decisive child is unique and special, just as every child is. It is very important not to label or judge their behaviors as good or bad. There is no best behavioral category. Every child has to learn new behaviors which will balance their natural behaviors. Every child's natural behaviors have disadvantages and advantages. Children need guidance understanding when their natural behaviors are an advantage and when they should use different, more appropriate behaviors according to the situation. In addition, children need to be affirmed and esteemed for their natural behaviors so they learn they are loved for who they are.

5

Talkative, Animated Children

Helen was considered popular in her sixth grade class. She had been voted the Class President and she was always asked to the birthday parties and other events her classmates hosted. Her family had recently joined a new church and Helen knew only two of the sixth-graders. Helen joined the Sunday evening youth group and appeared to enjoy her new friends. Several weeks passed. Then, after one of the youth meetings, Helen found her father in his car outside the church waiting for her. She opened the door, climbed in and burst into tears.

"Helen, what's wrong?" quizzed her father.

"I hate this church. Why did we ever have to change?" cried Helen.

"What happened? Tell me about it." encouraged her Father.

"No one likes me!" wailed Helen as more tears fell.

"Of course people like you, Honey," soothed her Father.

"No they don't, you're just saying that because you're my Dad," Helen's tears showed no signs of abating.

"What do you mean no one likes you? What happened to make you think that no one likes you?"

"They had elections tonight and ... and ..." Helen's voice gave way to sobs.

"And ..." prompted her father.

"I wasn't elected to ANYTHING!!!"

"Honey, you're still new to these kids. It may take some time before they know you," explained her Father.

"No, YOU DON'T UNDERSTAND! They had elections. There were seven offices to be filled. There were only ten kids at the meeting. THEY DON'T LIKE ME!"

Parents of the Talkative, Animated children from Category 2 may not be aware of how important approval is to their children. These children look for approval from everyone. They may experience great anxiety when they experience situations where they do not receive approval. For parents and teachers who do not have a need for approval, the reaction of these children may seem almost comical. Be assured that "approval" is a very serious matter to these children. When they think that others don't like them, their anxiety can overwhelm them. This anxiety can often be seen as an emotional reaction with the volume on loud. From one experience, such as being reprimanded by a parent, a young child with this behavioral style can declare, "Nobody loves me any more!" As the child grows and develops he may determine various ways of behaving to gain the approval and attention he desires. For example:

Cory finds new friends at the park where he plays by talking to children who are strangers. "He's absolutely amazing," says his mother. "Within minutes, Cory will know the child's name, what school he attends and how many siblings he has. I was never able to talk to children I didn't know when I was his age."

Joyce's Father explains how her need for approval has changed, "Joyce was always talkative and people-oriented. The kids and teachers usually seemed to really like her. But, when she got into Junior High we began to receive some negative comments from her teachers. Apparently she's turning into the class comedienne. She's got a great sense of humor and is able to get people to laugh. Frequently, she tells humorous stories about herself. But her need for approval by her peers is beginning to show up as lower grades and more teacher disapproval."

Six year old Larry and his family lived on a farm. Larry was ten years younger than his older brother, Neil, who worked after school and during the summer at a part-time job with a neighboring rancher. Larry's mother was frustrated with Larry's behavior.

"There's nothing to do," he would whine as he followed her from room to room. "Stop and play a game with me."

"Go outside and play on your swing or with your wagon, read a book, play with your toys; there's plenty to do," she'd respond.

What Larry's mother didn't understand about Larry was that as a Talkative, Animated child he said, "There's nothing to do." but he meant, "There's no one to play with."

In contrast to children with behavioral styles who prefer to be alone or want private time, the children from Behavioral Category 2 prefer being with others. They may not be able to imagine doing anything without having others involved.

Most children go through the childhood developmental phases when peer pressure becomes important. Most parents and teachers are aware that all children can be influenced by their peers. Every parent has probably heard the sentences: "But, Mom, everybody's got one." or "Dad, I have to go; everyone will be there." It is common for all children to be inclined to listen to their peer group. But, the children from Category 2 are naturally motivated to seek approval from their peers and others. This drive for approval can lead these children to believe that "only others have the power to make them O.K." They may not be able to separate "who they are" from what "others think about them." In a real sense, their joy or sorrow can depend on "what others think of them." Samatha's story illustrates this:

Samantha was so nervous that she forgot part of the cheer when she auditioned in front of her classmates. When the votes were counted, Samantha received the most votes and was head cheerleader for Junior Varsity. She was thrilled and she floated to class for the rest of the year knowing that "she was chosen" by everyone in the school. The next year, when she was a year older, she auditioned for a vacant spot on the Senior Varsity Squad. She didn't get the votes she needed. She was crushed. She thought no one liked her. She tried to figure out what she'd done wrong. She started being even nicer to people by giving even more compliments. She overheard someone in the restroom talking about her. The person said, "Samantha is so gushy, it makes me want to barf. You know she doesn't mean half of what she says." By now Samantha's anxiety was tipping the scale.

It is critical for parents and teachers to help these children learn ways of dealing with the anxiety they feel from loss of approval. It is dangerous for anyone to allow others to be in charge of his self-esteem. With guidance, these children will learn to value the feedback of others in appropriate proportion. In addition, it is critical these children learn to understand and accept their sense of "self" as separate from what others think about them.

Donna, who is now a successful sales consultant, was a Talkative, Animated child. She remembers how vital it was for her to receive the approval of others. She tells this story:

"I went to an all-girls Catholic school. We didn't have cheerleaders, so the symbol of popularity and prestige was to hold an office on the student council. I really wasn't interested in Government, but I knew that I had a good chance to be elected because I was popular. The way the elections operated was that everyone in the school voted once. The person with the most votes was declared the President. The person with the second most votes was declared the Vice-President and so on. When they started to announce the votes, I knew I had at least one of the offices. The announcements came over the school loudspeaker between classes. I was at my locker and Sister Veronica was talking with me when they announced the Treasurer. Since I wasn't the Treasurer, I knew I'd be either the Secretary, the Vice-President or the President. They announced the Secretary. Aretha was Secretary. The suspense was just killing me. I could hardly breathe. Then the announcement for Vice-President came over the loud speaker. It was Teresa McCarthy. Before they even announced my full name as President, I was screaming and crying. I remember the wonderful feeling that I was truly accepted and loved by everyone!! I was so overcome with emotion I was almost hysterical, when Sister Veronica whispered in my ear, 'It's not that big of a deal.' Her words brought me back to earth so that I could at least finish out the school day without crying."

The importance of gaining social approval and the anxiety of losing it can not be ignored in the life of Talkative, Animated children. These children must be guided to a more balanced understanding of the roles others play in their lives. They need to learn about how impossible it is to please everyone all the time. One of the ways to explain the impossibility of "getting everyone to like you" is to consider the four behavioral categories. It is totally unrealistic to think that anyone can meet the needs of all four styles at exactly the same time. For someone to meet the needs of a group of four people consisting of Category 1, 2, 3 and 4 behavioral styles, he would have to "take quick action," "talk," "allow things to remain the same," and allow time to "think" all at the same time. As an American President once said. "You can please all of the people some of the time and some of the people all of the time, but you can't please all of the people all of the time." Parents may want to esteem their Talkative, Animated children and guide them toward more balanced behaviors by saying things like:

"You are well liked by most of your classmates and that shows how well you get along with others. It is also important to like yourself. One of the ways we learn to like ourselves is to accept our differences. For example, I know that some people like to go to large parties. I am different. I like to go to small gatherings where there are close friends of mine. Your mother prefers to be alone sometimes. What do you like to do that is different from what your friends prefer to do?"

"I know you like to be with your friends and that's great. I'm glad you have the ability to get along with others. I also know that sometimes it is important to be able to stand alone. Let's talk about the situations when you may have to make different choices than your friends make. What if you were playing with your friends and they decided to throw rocks? What would be the best thing for you to say? What do you think would be the best thing for you to do? Would that be hard for you?"

"I know your friends are very important to you. You have good friends who like you. Sometimes friends change. When your friend Mark made the traveling fifth grade hockey team, he became very busy with the games. Just because you don't see him as much, it doesn't mean he doesn't like you."

"Sometimes situations cause changes. You may find new friends and sometimes you may have more distance with old friends. This is a natural part of life. It doesn't say anything about you. You are O.K. just the way you are."

"Your teacher says you are good at making your classmates laugh. It's O.K. to get attention by making others laugh in certain situations, like on the playground or when you're playing with your friends. However, you must use different behaviors in the classroom. Listening and paying attention to your work are important classroom behaviors."

Parents and teachers may be amazed by the emotional swings these Talkative, Animated children may exhibit. They live life emotionally. One minute they may be the happiest children on earth. The next minute they may be in the throes of depression. It may seem to parents and teachers that these children live life dramatically. They tend to involve themselves emotionally in everything they do. They put their heart into almost everything. Parents and teachers may find themselves persuaded by their emotional pleas. The following is a common dialogue in families with Talkative, Animated children:

Father

"Bedtime, Andrea, turn off the TV and go brush your teeth."

Andrea

"But, Daddy. This is the best movie. It's a wonderful movie about three dogs who get lost and then try to find their way home. PLEEESE, PLEASE. Let me finish it."

Father

"Tomorrow is a school day. Go get ready for bed."

Andrea

"If I get ready for bed really quick can I come back and watch for just 15 more minutes?"

Father

"No, tomorrow is a school day."

Andrea

Nearing tears, "But, Daddy, I have to know if the doggies make it home."

It may be hard to resist the heart-felt emotional pleas of these children. Remember, they can usually involve themselves emotionally in almost any situation. It is up to the parent or teacher involved to maintain the emotional objectivity to focus on the appropriate behavior. In the case of Andrea and the movie, her father knew his daughter well enough to know that her tears about missing the movie would be short-lived, but her fatigue from staying up an additional two hours would be more long lasting.

One disadvantage of the heart-felt emotional involvement is that these children may appear to others as insincere, gushy, mushy or clingy. Young children may smother their parents in hugs until the parents reach their hug saturation point. Having your child hug you can be a wonderful feeling. Having your child hang on you and hug you every few minutes can be frustrating. Parents don't want to discourage the child from demonstrating his love for them; they do, however, want to explain that other people's touching needs may be different than his. The amount of hugs and touching the child wants may be too much for others. Clear explanations about respecting the differences and wishes of others can help these children understand how to get positive approval from others.

Teachers report that young children from Category 2 appear to have their feelings hurt easily. These children truly do wear their hearts on their sleeves when it comes to emotional involvement. It is important for parents and teachers to understand how deeply these children feel. Adults may be inclined to say, "Oh, for heaven's sake, quit your crying." or "Don't be so foolish!" The situation may seem insignificant to an adult, but the child may truly be feeling heart-broken. The fact that the child recovers from the heart-break and an hour later is laughing, doesn't mean the feeling of heart-break wasn't real to the child.

Because these children are so emotionally involved, they may over-expend themselves emotionally, with the result that they experience an emotional overload. Uncontrollable crying, laughing hysterically, continuing to hug everyone in the room, acting maudlin and exhibiting excitement for a long period of time can all be symptoms of emotional fatigue. During these times of emotional fatigue, the child reaches an emotional saturation point and continues to engage in emotional involvement. The child is not able to successfully manage his emotional intensity and the emotions may overwhelm him. Parents and teachers will want to watch for symptoms of emotional fatigue and intervene by saying:

"We've been having such fun. Let's sit down together and just talk for a while."

"It is wonderful that you have such a good sense of humor and I like to hear you laugh. I also like to sit and be with you. Let's stop for a minute and catch our breath."

"Having fun and being excited is good. It's also good to balance excitement with times that are calm. Let's take a moment and be still and think about what we like about being calm."

"Emotions are like a swing. When you pump the swing high, you can feel the excitement. If you pump the swing too high it can be scary or the swing can start to go out of control. So it's important to understand when our emotions get too high or too low — just like the swing — we need to rest a moment — just like we'd do on the swing."

"When you are playing outside and you are feeling so excited that it starts to overwhelm you, remember to look around and notice things. Take a minute and look at the sky and see if you can see any shapes in the clouds."

To develop a long-term strategy for guiding these children, parents and teachers will need to consider coaching these children in the following areas: emotions, organization, time, conversation courtesy and carefulness. Parents will agree that all children have a range of emotions which they express. However, the Talkative, Animated children are motivated toward experiencing and expressing their emotions more than any of the other styles. The advantage of this is that these children have the ability to express their emotions. They can tell someone how much they love him. They become enthusiastic about people and situations. Enthusiasm is a wonderful quality which can motivate people. Their enthusiasm and excitement is often catching. The disadvantage of this emotional focus is that these children may miss the facts. Their subjective feelings and hunches may become their reality regardless of the events. Parents will need to help them balance their feelings with the facts. The following is an example of a Talkative, Animated child who allowed her friendly feelings to guide her actions:

Parent

Getting out of the shower, "Who were you just talking to?"

Child

Cheerfully, "Oh this nice man came to the door and wanted to know if we wanted to buy some magazines. I told him that you were in the shower and that Mrs. Wilson, across the street, is usually home at this time. He's going to talk to her and then come back and see us. He told me he has a daughter my age and she has a playhouse. He built it for her. She lives in Kansas with her mom when he's working."

Parent

"We have a rule about opening the door to strangers."

Child

"Oh, but this man isn't a stranger. When I was playing with Sally yesterday, he stopped and talked with us. Sally's mom even bought a magazine."

These children are friendly with almost everyone and strongly rely on their subjective feelings. This, coupled with their innate trust of others, makes them comfortable with all types of people, even strangers. Parents and teachers will have to insist these children follow the basic safety rules even if they "feel" there is no danger.

Parents need to continually esteem their Talkative, Animated children for their emotional sensitivity, while guiding them toward a more balanced objective viewpoint. It is important to honor their feelings. Remember, their feelings may make up much of their subjective view of their world. At the same time, it is critical that parents and teachers ask the type of questions which guide these children toward considering the facts of the situation. In the following dialogue, Beth is focused only on her feelings until her mother coaches her.

Sixteen year old Beth in tears

"I looked horrible. No one liked me."

Parent

"What happened?"

Beth

"My life is ruined. That's what happened!"

Parent

Gently, "Can you tell me about the situation?"

Beth

"Well, Allison came up to me at the intermission and said, 'What do you think casual means? You look like you just stepped out of an ad for lipstick.' "

Parent

"Then what happened?"

Beth

"What do you mean, 'Then what happened?' That's it! I was too dressed up. They thought I was stuck up."

Parent

"What was everyone wearing?"

Beth

"Jeans mostly; a couple of girls wore shorts."

Parent

"And you were wearing jeans too, right?"

Beth

"Yea, but the top I was wearing was kinda fancy."

Parent

"What kind of tops were the other girls wearing?"

Beth

"Well, Mary had on a sweater and Nicole had on a long-sleeved shirt with a vest. It was a great vest. Her mom brought it back from India. I wish I could figure out how to find one like it."

Parent

"It sounds like Nicole was a little dressed up. What was Allison wearing?"

Beth
"She had on a T-shirt with a funny saying; something like 'my parents went to Hawaii and all they brought back was this lousy shirt.' "
Parent
"So Allison was the only one in a T-shirt?"
Beth
"Oh, you mean maybe she didn't like what she wore so she said something about me."

Bill did not get the coaching that Beth did. His experience was very painful for him:

Late one afternoon some seventh grade boys were horsing around after school as they waited for the bus. Freshly fallen snow covered the ground with the perfect material for making snow balls. The seven boys began throwing snowballs at the side of the building. After the first snowball stuck to the side of the building, they had a target. The objective of the game was to get your snowball to stick to the side of the building as near as possible to the first snowball. Grunting, the boys put muscle into each throw. A car pulled up and Bill's father called to him from the driver's seat. As Bill and his father drove off, a teacher walked out the school door and pulled the boys into detention. Unknown to the boys, detention was being held on the other side of their snowball target. Each thud of a snowball had sounded like a small explosion in the enclosed room. After some questioning, the boys admitted that Bill had thrown the first snowball. When Bill arrived at school the next day, the detention teacher was waiting to serve him with a detention notice. What neither his parents nor his teachers realized was the detention never fazed Bill; what broke his heart was that he thought "his friends didn't like him." As an adult, Bill still remembers and talks about the intense hurt he felt when it appeared to him that his friends had rejected him. The reality of the facts or how it happened cannot compete with the "feeling of rejection" Bill experienced.

Beth, Bill and other Talkative, Animated children of Category 2 need ongoing guidance to develop a more objective

view of others and ways of coping with the natural rejections
children experience. This guidance is most effective in the form
of conversation. Because these children love to talk, parents
and teachers can use specific questions to guide these children
to their own understanding of the facts. Parents and teachers
must be aware of how easily these children may feel hurt and
not use the conversation to make light of their feelings. In
contrast, adults do not want to make too much out of their
feelings either. Instead, the focus must be on gently
determining the facts. Parents and teachers can help the
Talkative, Animated child develop more objectivity just by asking
different questions. For example, instead of asking the child
how he likes something, ask him to describe it. Or, ask
questions in such a way that you encourage the child to develop
his skills of observation. Although the child may enjoy his
observation skills, it will ask him to focus on "thinking" instead of
"feeling." These types of questions and encouragement can
help the child begin to develop more objectivity. In the following
situation, a day at the park offers a parent some coaching
opportunities with his Talkative, Animated child:

Child

"What a wonderful day. This is the best day I've
ever had."

Parent

"I'm glad you are having a good time. I like having
fun with you. Tell me, what is it that you like about
today?"

Child

"Everything! I love being in the park with you. I love
you. You're the best daddy in the world."

Parent

"You said you love being in the park. Look around
the park and tell me what you see."

Child

"I see trees ... millions of trees and I see grass ...
lots of grass ... and there's a bench and people ...
lots of friendly people."

Parent

"Are all the trees the same or can you see
differences in the trees?"

Child

"Some trees are big. Some trees are little. Some aren't trees at all, are they? That one over there isn't a tree."

Parent

"You're right. That's not a tree. It's a lilac bush. I have an idea, let's gather the leaves from under the trees and see how many different kinds of leaves we can find."

In addition to using conversation to help the child develop more objectivity, parents and teachers can help the child learn to vary his attention from his emotions to his surrounding environment and his body. By asking the child to listen to his breathing, you move him away from his emotional focus and toward a focus on breath. By asking the child to notice his surroundings and make note of the shapes and colors, you are teaching the child to move from his emotional focus to a more objective focus.

"Breaks" and planned quiet times can be helpful for these children when they begin to be overwhelmed by their emotions. Because these children become so emotionally involved, they can become emotionally depleted with no defenses, patience or negotiation skills left. A planned quiet period which temporarily removes them from other people gives these children time to recover. Because involvement with others often gives these children an emotional "high" which can climb out of control, parents and teachers can use "emotional breaks" to help these children manage their behaviors.

These children may try to follow the rules about picking up clothes and putting dishes in the sink. When they are stressed, they may be very disorganized. The child may leave a messy room or forget to comb his hair. As parents and teachers will attest, these children are not the most naturally organized children. Even on their best days, they may not have the attention to maintain all their papers in an organized manner. But when they are in stressful situations, it can get even worse. Helping these children understand the importance of organization and how to keep track of books and school work is a worthy goal for parents and teachers. They may have to specifically explain that a notebook has five pockets, one for each class in the day. By keeping homework in the right pocket, the child can be assured that the paper will not be lost. But, if a friend talks to him right after the bell rings before the paper is put in the correct pocket, there's still a chance that the paper will be misplaced while he focuses on talking to his friend. Remember, for these children, people will usually be more important than the task. Parents and teachers can guide these children toward a more balanced view of tasks by announcing the rules or guidelines before the child emotionally engages in a situation. The consequences for ignoring tasks must be appropriate, depending on the child's age. Parents may say something like:

"If you misplace your homework, you will have to redo it all."

"If you forget your books at home, you will have to go through the day without books."

"If you forget to come home on time because you get so involved with the other kids, you will have to play alone at home the next two days."

"If you don't clean up your room by Friday, you will lose your telephone privileges for the weekend."

In order to understand these unique children's perception of time, parents and adults must understand their ability to interact fully in the moment. One parent tells this example of how time was perceived by her teenage daughter:

"I sent Melissa to the grocery story for milk. The grocery story is about four miles from our house and Melissa had recently gotten her driver's license. I thought it would be a good way to let her 'solo' for a short time. Two hours later, I was almost ready to call the police when Melissa waltzed in with the milk. I accused her of driving around and not coming straight home. But she assured me that she'd only driven to the grocery store. She met several people she knew and talked to them for a few minutes. Without her realizing it, her few minutes turned into an hour and a half!"

These children view "interacting with someone in the present" as the time priority. Being able to focus on the present and the individual you are interacting with is most definitely an advantage. In certain situations, it is also a disadvantage. The disadvantage occurs when the child is so focused on "talking to his friends" that he forgets his homework. These children need guidance in how to set goals and how to develop a plan to meet them, while still having time to be with friends. Without a plan and adult guidance, these children will want to meet their teacher's objectives, but they may end up just enjoying their classmates.

Because these children are natural communicators, people believe they will do well in any situation with people. However, these children's natural drive to talk, to be enthusiastic and to "be in the spotlight" may work against them with some individuals. Others may see this talkativeness as controlling or even selfish. When the Animated, Talkative child is the only one who gets to talk in class, his classmates may resent his "hogging the attention." Because the Talkative, Animated child is so verbally quick, he may interrupt others, or always be the first to talk. Because he is so enthusiastic and playful, others may see him as flippant or insincere when he jokes with them. Therefore, these children need to be esteemed for their behaviors and reminded about conversation courtesy. For example, a parent or teacher might say:

"It's great that you are so verbally quick and it's important to make sure others get a chance to talk."

"I know you have good ideas and you often can say funny things that make people laugh. This is good. It is also good to let others talk without interrupting. When you interrupt someone they may not like that behavior."

"I know you can think of hundreds of things to say that are witty and funny. That's one of your best advantages. It is also important to let other people talk."

"You have a real talent for expressing yourself in words and I know you like people. After you say something, be sure that you take a break and let other people express their ideas too."

"It's good to be talkative and expressive. Because you are so verbally quick, others may think that you are "hogging the show." Make sure that you stop and think: Has everyone gotten a chance to talk? Have others been doing some of the talking? If you answer 'No,' then be sure to ask a question so that someone else has a chance to talk."

Because these children tend to focus on people, they may not offer enough attention to their responsibilities. According to the child's age, parents must outline their responsibilities and take time to talk about the importance of getting "things" done; things like making the bed, remembering their homework, taking out the trash and making their school lunch. Because these children do not have a natural tendency to organize their tasks, they will need help organizing and maintaining ways of keeping on top of their responsibilities. These children usually want to please their teachers and parents. Remember, they want to be liked by everyone and they like to be involved. So an easy way to get them started understanding their chores is to talk about them or initially do the chore with them. For a young child, a parent could say, "Your toys belong to you. When you're not playing with them at night, they should be in your toy box. So every night we'll use this laundry basket and together we'll pick them up." For an older child, instead of saying, "You have to clean your room on Saturday morning," a parent may want to involve the child in a group cleaning effort. A parent could say, "On Saturday morning we have to clean the bedrooms, so let's work together. It will go faster and we'll be able to talk while we clean. Plan two hours for cleaning. Then you'll be able to get together with friends."

As you read through the description of the Talkative, Animated Children, it is very important that you do not label or judge these behaviors as good or bad. There is no best behavioral type. Each behavioral category has advantages and disadvantages. Each child has to learn new behaviors to be more effective. Every child needs guidance on how to moderate and balance his natural behaviors with new, learned behaviors. In addition, each child needs to be affirmed and esteemed for his natural behaviors so that he learns that he is O.K. – that he is loved for who he is.

6

Soft-Spoken, Cooperative Children

Joey was happily following his morning routine. He was dressed, hair combed, bed made and getting his cereal bowl out of the cupboard when he asked,

"Why isn't Daddy at breakfast?"

"Because he needs to sleep in. Remember, I told you last night that he was going to work at night for a while. He works until early in the morning and doesn't get up until you're at morning recess," explained Joey's mother.

"But ... but" Joey gulped tearfully, "he always eats breakfast with me and kisses me good-bye."

Anything that changes the normal routine of the Soft-spoken, Cooperative child is upsetting. These children need the security of predictable occurrences. They derive great comfort and security from knowing there is a pattern to living. Getting up every morning at 8:00 is not a chore for these children. If 8:00 is the normal time they arise, they will feel comforted by the "sameness" of getting up at the regular time each day. These children are motivated to preserve the same daily and weekly conditions. They are contented when they know they have a system of predictable events in their lives, such as:

Monday

Get up at 7:00. Get dressed. Have breakfast. Brush teeth. Catch the bus at 8:15. Reading class at 9:30. Recess at 10:45. Lunch at 12:15. Math class at 1:30. Recess at 2:15. Music or art class at 3:00. Catch the bus at 3:40. Get a snack. Do chores. Have dinner. Do homework. Watch TV. Brush teeth. Go to bed at 9:00.

Tuesday

Get up at 7:00. Get dressed. Have breakfast. Brush teeth. Catch the bus at 8:15. Reading class at 9:30. Recess at 10:45. Lunch at 12:15. Math class at 1:30. Recess at 2:15.

Music or art class at 3:00. Catch the bus at 3:40. Go to a friend's house to play. Get picked up at 5:30. Have dinner. Do homework. Watch TV. Brush teeth. Go to bed at 9:00.

Sunday

Get up at 7:00. Read newspaper funnies with mom. Get dressed for Sunday school. Go to children's Sunday school class at 9:30. Stop for donuts at the cafe. Go home. Change clothes. Go for a walk with Uncle Harry. Have lunch at 1:00 with family relatives. Help clear the table and wash the dishes. Play a game with cousins. Do homework. Watch TV. Brush teeth. Go to bed at 9:00.

For the Soft-spoken, Cooperative child an ongoing schedule like this offers contentment. If dad or mom needs to change the schedule because of job considerations or other conditions, the Soft-spoken, Cooperative child may experience some anxiety. When their routine is disturbed, they may perceive the disturbance as evidence of "something wrong." This sense of "wrong-ness" can cause tears, anger and other types of behaviors which seem uncommon for these normally easy-going, unflappable children. It is important to understand that these children will need special guidance before certain types of situations occur. The following are just a few of the types of situations which will impact the routine of the Soft-spoken, Cooperative child:

• Christmas, Easter, Birthdays or any holiday that will affect the child's regular pattern of doing things.

• The birth, adoption or arrival of any new family member.

• The starting or stopping of the school year.

• Moving to a new house, even in the same area.

• Graduation or changing schools.

• A change in friends.

• A new church or joining any organization as a new member.

• The death of a pet, family member, teacher or acquaintance.

• A change of a parent's schedule in cases such as in new jobs, new classes, new responsibilities.

• Any duty parents accept which changes the amount of time or way they spend their time at home.

Of course, all children may have some anxiety to changes in their lives. But, the Soft-spoken, Cooperative children have anxiety and discomfort with even small changes. The larger life changes may become highly stressful. Parents and teachers can help these children by explaining:

"I know the changes which disrupt your everyday life are sometimes uncomfortable for you. It's nice to have the happiness that comes from knowing what's going to happen. AND, sometimes there are changes. When you go to school next year, you will still get up and get dressed before you eat breakfast, just like you always do. Then a bus will come for you. In the beginning ... the first time you ride the bus it may feel uncomfortable because things are different. I know the feeling of being uncomfortable will go away and soon you will like the feeling of knowing that the bus will be waiting for you every morning. You can be sure that a bus will be waiting for you. And ... some day just knowing that the bus will be there, will also bring you a feeling of comfort."

"In a month, I will be changing jobs. That means there will be some changes around the house. What isn't going to change is: you will still get up at the same time and follow the same routine until you get to school. There is much that will remain the same. And, there will be some things which will feel different until we get comfortable with them. After school, you will not come home like you did before. Instead, you will go to grandma's house. She is so happy you'll be staying with her after school until I come to pick you up. The things that will remain the same are: after school you will still have a snack and then you will practice your flute and then you will do your homework. What is different is that you will do it at grandma's house."

"In a few weeks school will be out for summer break, so some of your routine will be different. In the beginning, having a different routine may feel strange, but soon you'll discover how much fun you'll be able to have in the summer. Let's talk about the some of the changes the summer will bring and some of the things that will remain the same."

These children are most comfortable having things remain the same. Because of this motivation for "sameness," they may want to keep everything: old toys they don't play with, old books, old clothes they can't wear and even school papers from years ago. Throwing one of these items away means letting go of the familiar and by extrapolation, opening to the unfamiliar. Parents may be stunned by the amount of storage they will need to maintain these children's accumulated items. One loving father tells of the incredible feat he accomplished to help his daughter retain an item which she didn't want to leave:

"We decided to sell the farm and move to town. My twelve year old daughter, Rebecca, grieved the change so much, I tried to comfort her by talking about it. I said, 'Rebecca, by living in town you'll have more opportunity to be with your friends. You'll see how much you'll like it, if you just give it a chance.'

She agreed with me but added, 'Daddy, I just hate leaving.'

So I asked her, 'What do you hate leaving the most?'

After some thought she replied, 'Don't laugh, Daddy.'

She made me promise, 'I won't laugh.'

Then she quietly explained 'Well ... I'm going to miss that large flat rock. I've played on it as long as I can remember. Sometimes it was a boat. Sometimes it was a castle. Daddy, ever since I was a little girl I've always sat on it. The sun warms it and I like to sit there every night after dinner in the spring and fall. In the summer, I like to eat lunch there sometimes, like a picnic. And in the winter I sweep the snow off. I don't know why Daddy, but when I think about not having that rock to sit on I ... I ... I feel so lost. I know it sounds so silly. But that's what I hate leaving the most, even more than leaving my room.'

Without thinking I dreamed out loud, 'If we could take the rock with us and put it in the back yard, would that make this change easier for you?'

'Oh, YES! YES! It would make everything so much easier,' she exclaimed.

A few days later, I explained to my wife I planned to move a rock which weighed around two tons to our backyard. She thought I was a little crazy to do it. But I understood how important it was to my little girl. Things like that old rock are symbols of our history ... our past ... and when the whole world seems to always be changing, there is a solace in something solid from the past."

Not every child will have such an understanding father. Not every Soft-spoken child will want a two-ton rock, but most will find it difficult to throw away anything from the past. Keeping those items gives them comfort in an ever-changing world. For the adults who are interacting with these children, it will be critical to remember that the Soft-spoken, Cooperative children will need guidance and time to adjust to changes which occur in their lives.

Parents and teachers may identify these children by their persistence in doing things. These children can occupy their time making doll clothes, drawing the rooms of an imaginary play house, building roads for their trucks and a myriad of other projects. They may especially like toys which create a "task to do," such as toys which build something. In contrast to the Active, Decisive children who like to see "results" from their actions, the Soft-spoken, Cooperative children enjoy the process of being absorbed in the task at hand. Adults may be surprised at the persistence and hard work these children bring to their projects. They often outlast other children, as Gerry did in the following situation:

Seth
"Gerry, let's take a break; it's taking forever to put this together."

Gerry
"I just want to finish putting the tires on the car. You go ahead. Mom said there are cookies for us in the kitchen."

Seth
"I brought you a cookie. I ate mine and called my mom to let her know I was still here. Let's go out and shoot some baskets."

Gerry
"Aw, let's just finish with the glue. O.K.? Look, it's starting to take shape. Isn't it a great looking RX 7?

We're almost ready to put on the decals. Do you want to start them while I glue the last part?"
Seth
"I guess."

When other children have tired of the project, these Soft-spoken, Cooperative children are often still working. They have the ability to keep a constant work rhythm. Gerry liked the pace and the process of "putting the car together" and he experienced a sense of satisfaction seeing the concrete results of completing his project. Children like Gerry prefer tangible rewards; concrete things they can see. Teachers will recognize these children as the ones who excel when the lesson involves "hands on" examples of the theories. Most children enjoy learning when they are involved in experiencing the theories. But, these children usually need a direct relationship between tasks and the material being taught.

Because these children tend to be modest about themselves and their accomplishments, they rarely risk having classmates taunt them with statements like, "Stuck up!" or "She thinks she's better than everyone else." Their unassuming, easy-going nature usually eases them into positive interactions with a range of children. They may be so modest and unassuming that they aren't noticed, as was the case with Margy in the following dialogue:
Mom, eating dinner
"I'm glad you did so well on your spelling test, Ricky."
Seven year old Ricky
"I also got a compliment from the bus driver. He said he'd never seen anyone who was as happy as I am. He said he likes my smile!"
Mom
"How about you, Margy? You haven't said much. Are you excited about the championship basketball game you're playing tomorrow?"
Eleven year old Margy
"Yeah. I guess so."
Mom
"Are you nervous?"

Margy
"No."
Ricky
"You'll never guess what Alan Johnson did today. The teacher was so mad. She sent him to the principal."

Even though Margy's basketball team made it to the championship finals, the total attention she received for it at dinner was one question. Margy's modesty and Soft-spoken nature may make it challenging to draw her out and give her more recognition. Often parents assume, incorrectly, that these children do not want praise, as in the example of the twins, Cathy and Cory. Their father told this story:

"Both Cathy and Cory entered a coloring contest sponsored by the local newspaper. I never thought they'd win, but one morning I received a call from the newspaper informing me that Cathy had won first place and Cory won second place. The first place prize was a camera and the second place prize was a painting set. I asked them to wait before they announced it. Then I talked it over with my wife. We agreed to ask the newspaper to announce that Cory had won first place. You see, Cory is so competitive there'd be no peace in the house if Cathy won first place and ... Cathy's so easy-going she doesn't appear to care about it ... at least not the way Cory does. We called and explained it to the newspaper and they agreed to reverse the order. Everyone was happy. Cory and Cathy will never know who really won first place."

Modest children like Cathy are frequently overlooked when it comes to the rewards and appreciation they need. Because they are quiet and unassuming does not mean they don't have needs for recognition. These children want and need sincere appreciation from the adults in their lives. The parents and teachers who say, "Good job," may interpret the quiet reaction from these children as disinterest. Nothing could be further from the truth. Adults may not see the "internal beaming of pleasure" which Soft-spoken children experience when they are offered sincere appreciation for who they are and for the good work they do. Even though these children may gently disagree with the compliment, they want and need the sincere recognition. Even if the compliments appear not to be heard, parents and teachers must continue to give positive recognition such as:

> "Billy, you did so well at the concert. It's the best I've heard you play your recital piece."
>
> "Aw, I don't know."
>
> "I think you did really well. I'm so proud of you."
>
> "Umm."
>
> "I think we should celebrate with a stop at the ice cream store. What kind of ice cream should we have for our celebration?"
>
> "Chocolate?"
>
> "Then chocolate it is!"

The Soft-spoken children will need special guidance in the areas of: finding new, shorter ways of doing things, understanding change, finding new friends and activities, telling others their thoughts and feelings, developing firmness and an ability to say "no" and developing an open attitude toward new ideas and controversy.

Because these children like to have a routine or a system for doing things, they often are committed to doing things the same way even though the situation may have changed. A young child may not want to take the next step toward being grown up, if it means that she has to give up her old routine. Everything from bottles and baths to food may have a certain routine which the child likes. Conversations about developing new, quicker ways of doing things may sound like:

Mother
> "Honey, it will be faster if I make the beds while you make the pancakes. You're old enough to cook the pancakes now, without help from me."

Julie
> "But, we always make pancakes together on Saturdays."

Mother
> "I know, but this will make everything go faster. We'll finish breakfast and some cleaning and we'll be able to go to the park sooner."

Julie

"I don't want to go to the park sooner. Let's make pancakes like we always do, please."

*   *   *

Father

"Now that you're older, you can walk to school with your friends. What do you think of that?"

Mike

"They always cut through the Industrial Park."

Father

"There are good sidewalks there. Is there something about the Industrial Park that bothers you?"

Mike

"No, it's just that you always walked me to school down the street with the huge trees and the huge houses. I like looking at the houses. Remember, in December, how they decorated the houses?"

Father

"I'm sure your friends like the fact that by cutting through the Industrial Park you walk two blocks less. You'll be home faster."

Mike

"I liked walking to school the old way."

*   *   *

Classmate

"John, let me help you. Here's a faster way to do your math, look."

John

"I like the way we did it last year."

Classmate

"I know, but that's so slow. That's how the little kids do it. Look how much faster this is. Isn't this great?"

John

Hesitantly, "Yeah, I guess so."

*   *   *

Coach

"O.K. Boys, quiet down. Mr. Wallace is going to
show you how to make that swimming turn faster.
Last year we turned laterally. This new turn is
almost like a dive. You'll push off from the wall and
stay under water as you complete the turn."

Later, Coach talking alone to Jeff

"Jeff, everyone seems to like the new turn. What do
you think of it?"

Jeff

"I guess it's O.K."

Coach

"Really, you don't seem very enthusiastic. Please
tell me what you're thinking. I can tell you're not
very excited about it. Can you tell me why?"

Jeff

"Why can't we just do it like we did last year?"

Coach

"Well, for one reason this turn is faster. And another
reason, it's always good to learn new things, don't
you think so?"

Jeff

"Yeah, I guess so." Talking to himself, "I like the
turn we used last year."

Parents and teachers may need to encourage the Soft-
spoken child to accept new ways of doing things. Remember,
these children get comfortable with a routine or system of how
they do things and they may need guidance in understanding
why things have to change. In guiding Jeff, the swimmer, the
Coach will want to acknowledge Jeff's reluctance to change:

Coach

"Jeff, I think you like the turn we did last year better,
is that right?"

Jeff

"Maybe."

Coach

"Well, I think the turn we used last year worked
really well for you. I know when something works

well for you it must be hard to consider something new. What I'd like you to do is just have fun and try this new turn for four weeks. After four weeks you and I will sit down and talk about which is the best turn for you to use. But, during the four weeks, I want you to try your best with the new turn so that you can make a good comparison between the two. Will you do that?"

Jeff

"O.K. But what if I like the old turn when we talk."

Coach

"That's what we'll talk about. We'll look at your times with the new turn and see if you are beginning to like it. If not, we'll talk about what you can do. Is it a deal?"

Jeff

"Deal!"

Four weeks of practice with the new turn developed a sense of routine and comfort for Jeff. By the time he talked with the coach, he had already begun to develop a routine with the new turn.

When it comes to changing their routines or changing the way they do things, parents and teachers may be surprised at the incredible stubbornness these easy-going children can display. Normally these children prefer to take their time, especially in the context of any change, but if an adult pushes them, the quiet, stubborn response may be surprising. Adults need to be cautioned about prodding their child's quiet stubbornness. Patience with these children will usually yield higher results. Parents and teachers have reported that these Soft-spoken children, when pushed, will listen quietly and even seem to agree before returning to the old way of doing it. To circumvent this stubborn response, adults will need some skill. Remember, pushing the child to change usually will not work. Instead, parents and teachers can ask the child to "test pilot" the new way for a few weeks. It is unlikely at the end of four weeks the child will still prefer the old way. Four weeks is enough time to develop a comfort with a new routine. But, if at the end of four weeks the child still desires the old way, parents and teachers may want to respect her choice in select situations.

Because these children like the old and the familiar, they may need gentle encouragement when it comes to new activities and new friends. Although these children are cooperative in almost any work group, they will usually select a small group of friends who will be "friends forever." Often their commitment to their select group of friends eliminates the opportunity for new friendships to form. Parents and teachers can provide opportunities for new friendships to develop by creating a structure for the Soft-spoken, Cooperative children to interact with new children over a period of time. These interactions will build comfort and a sense of history with the new person who may eventually become a friend. Teachers can create new work groups which last at least a month. Daily interactions during the month will allow the Soft-spoken, Cooperative child an opportunity to develop a shared history with children with whom she usually would not play. Parents may want to ask families to be part of a "weekly gathering." With structured games and activities these children can be encouraged to engage with more children than just their small group of friends.

When it comes to new activities, these children will naturally prefer the old and comfortable things they do. Parents and teachers can teach these children the joy of trying new things by making "trying new things" a family or classroom norm. The following examples offer some ideas about creating a new norm.

Father at a family meeting: "I know we like to do the same things on the weekend. I think it's great that we do things together. What I'd like to suggest is, we pick one night a month to try something new, as a family. One night we could try bowling. One night we could take a drive to a park we haven't seen. It doesn't have to take a lot of time or money, but one night a month ... let's try something new. And, I'd like everyone to make suggestions for what things we should try together."

Teacher speaking to her class: "I know everyone has favorite things they like to do during free time. We all have favorites and that's good. And, sometimes it's good to try something new. Two days a month during free time, I will announce a 'Day to try new things.' Then everyone will get ten minutes extra time to try something they haven't done before. On these days, I will bring in some new books and games to ensure that everyone gets to try something new. Then as a class we'll discuss what things you liked best."

Teachers will find the following four part strategy useful with the Soft-spoken, Cooperative children. First, it is important to be sincere. These children respond to heart-felt sincerity. The genuine, unfeigned warmth the child feels from her teacher will be the basis for trust and communication. Where other children may like a teacher who is funny and cracks jokes or a teacher who teases, the Soft-spoken child responds to sincerity. The second part of the strategy is not to push the child, but to use patience and let the child warm up to the situation in her own time. Teachers often think a little push will get faster results, but with the Soft-spoken, Cooperative child, pushing will almost certainly slow down the process. Third, allow time for their communications. These children will not communicate as fast or as fully as an adult would prefer. It will take time and gentle questions for the teacher to develop a relationship with these children. The final part of the strategy deals with how to effectively teach Soft-spoken children. They learn best when the information is organized with specific steps. Outlines, sequences and procedures which are listed out in a step by step format will appeal to the routine which these children prefer.

Parents and teachers may perceive the Soft-spoken, Cooperative children are reluctant to talk about their feelings or thoughts. Actually, it's not reluctance the parents and teachers are seeing, but a different communication style. These children may not be motivated to talk a great deal. When they do talk, they will usually suggest or infer. It is rare for children of Behavioral Category 3 to be as direct or straightforward as some of the children from Behavioral Categories 1 and 2. Because these children usually give small parts of information in response to questions, parents and teachers may be receiving only half of the story, as in the situation with Dianna:

Teacher talking to seven year old Dianna
"Dianna, everyone has finished their paper but you. Why aren't you finished?"
Dianna
"I couldn't finish it."

Teacher
"What do you mean? Was it too hard?"
Dianna
Tentatively, "No."
Teacher
"Well if it wasn't too hard, why didn't you do your work?"
Dianna
"I couldn't get it done."
Teacher
"Dianna, are you feeling alright? This isn't like you. Are you sick?"
Dianna
"No, ... it's just that ... I couldn't do it."
Teacher
"Dianna, I really want to understand what is happening here. Can you explain it to me?"
Dianna
Tears forming in her eyes, whispering, "no."
Lorraine
"Teacher, I know what's wrong with Dianna. She told me her kitty died this morning. She cried on the bus all the way to school."

Like Dianna, the Soft-spoken child may have difficulty telling her feelings. She would rather listen than talk and she may appear to "beat around the bush" when parents or teachers ask direct questions. Parents and teachers will need patience when asking these children to communicate with them. When adults allow time for the child to get comfortable with both the adult and the topic of conversation, they will get more information. But, adults will have to show the child that she will not be pushed or punished and that she has the time she needs to get comfortable so she can share her thoughts and feelings. Parents and teachers will have to listen closely to these children, as they will say much through their "suggestions and inferences," such as in the following illustration:
Mother
"Jack and Cindy, I want to thank you both for cleaning the house today after school. You each did chores which will really help me. It looks

wonderful. You'll both get the rewards I promised you. Thank you for your hard work."

Cindy
"Well, I did work a long time."

Mother
"And I really appreciate it. You are both great."

Cindy
"Uh, I think I worked a little longer than Jack."

Mother
"Well, Cindy, everything isn't always fair. The important thing is that all the work got done. Don't you agree?"

Cindy, telephone ringing as she speaks,
"I guess so."

Mother
"Yes ... he's here. Oh, he did? No, I didn't know. Well, thank you, Margaret. Yes, I'm glad you called."

Mother, talking to Jack,
"That was Mrs. Krachna. She was calling to make sure you'd made it home safely, since you didn't leave her house until after dark. She said you came home from school with Stan and played basketball in the driveway until it got too dark to shoot baskets. Is that right?"

Jack
"Yeah Mom, I forgot. I would have cleaned the house if I remembered. Honest."

Mother
"Cindy, why didn't you tell me you did all the work yourself? Jack was getting credit for your hard work."

Cindy
"I did tell you."

In the situation with Jack and Cindy, Cindy tried to suggest to her mother that Jack had not done his share of work when she said, "I think I worked a little longer than Jack." To understand Cindy's motivation, remember, she needs to cooperate with others. She may feel Jack took unfair advantage of her, but that doesn't negate her need to get along and cooperate with Jack and her mother. Parents and teachers may see this behavior as lacking assertiveness. To help these children develop more balanced behaviors in terms of cooperativeness and assertiveness, it is important for parents and teachers to reinforce the positive work initiative while coaching these children in more direct communication. For example, Cindy's mother could say:

Mother

"I am so happy that you took the initiative to clean the house. You are to be commended for your good work habits and your commitment to get all the cleaning done. When you do good work like this, I really want to know. Can you see how you did a larger job than we originally planned for you? By doing Jack's work and yours, you really did a lot more. When you do extra effort, I want you to tell me. Do you think we could have a 'secret code?' When you do extra work and I don't see it, could you say to me, 'There's extra!' And whenever you say that, I'll know there is more than meets the eye. Can that be our secret code?"

Cindy

"Yes "

Mother

"And, whenever you think I'm not hearing your whole message, will you use the code 'there's extra.' 'There's extra' will mean to me that I'm not hearing some of the message you're trying to tell me."

When Cindy alerts her mother that there is extra information, her mother will be in a prime position to ask questions and coach Cindy toward how to explain more of her thoughts and feelings. In addition to coaching about more direct communications, Cindy will need guidance on assertiveness. She will need to learn how to say "no" and be firm. This is not a small task for children like Cindy. Of all the behavioral styles, these children are the most naturally influenced by others. Because of their quiet communication which "suggests" and doesn't "tell," other people may see these children as "easily influenced" and apply pressure, as in the situation with Harry and Ted.

Harry
>"Come on Ted. Let's go to the *Batman* movie."

Ted
>"Well, I thought we'd agreed to see the cowboy film."

Harry
>"Yeah, I know, but that was before we knew that this one was playing. Come on, this one will be better."

Ted
>"My mom said she'd pick us up at the movie when it was over ... ."

Harry
>"So, we'll just run the three blocks back here when the show's out. It's no big deal. Come on, you coming or not?"

Ted
>"Oh well, awww, I don't know."

Harry
>"Ted, come on. We're going to miss the start. You're gonna make us late. You coming?"

Ted
>"I guess."

Parents and teachers may have to design scenarios and help their Soft-spoken children role play saying "no" and showing "firmness." Parents and teachers can make a game out of the instruction by playing "let's pretend." For example, a parent driving to the grocery story with his Soft-spoken, Cooperative child could say:

>"Let's play a game. I call it "let's pretend." Let's pretend that a friend is playing at our house. You want to play with your trucks. Your friend wants to play a board game. Now, sometimes it's good to let your friend have his choice. But let's pretend the last time you played together your friend got to choose what to do. That means it's your turn to choose. Let's pretend that you say 'Let's play with the trucks.' and your friend says 'No, we're going play a board game.' Now, together we can figure out what you can say and then we can try it. What do you think a good thing to say would be?"

Teachers can have children "act out the parts" in situations where a classmate is trying to push another classmate to do something she doesn't want to do. With this type of guidance and coaching the Soft-spoken, Cooperative children will learn new behaviors which they can choose to use. It's important to understand that even with the exposure to new assertive behaviors these children will still prefer to cooperate most of the time. But an exposure to assertive behaviors will allow the child to have a choice of behaviors.

When it comes to new ideas and controversy, these children may exhibit a very closed attitude. Controversy, arguments, debate and conflict will all increase the anxiety of these Soft-spoken children. Remember, they want cooperation and in their understanding of the world, controversy, arguments, debate and conflict are representative of people NOT cooperating. Thus, it can be critical for parents and teachers to help these children understand the benefit of disagreements. Teachers can reinforce the concept of debates and disagreements as a natural way people learn from each other and develop better solutions as in the following example:

"When the work team couldn't decide what step to take next, I noticed some of you getting uncomfortable. Sometimes it is important for people to disagree so that they come up with better ideas. When people disagree, more than one idea is looked at. Frequently, we can learn from each other and come up with better ways of doing things. Many of you have probably heard of the saying, 'two heads are better than one.' Well, in fact, two heads are better than one when they are disagreeing about an idea and working to come up with better ideas."

Parents can explain the importance of understanding how disagreements benefit members of the family by saying something like:

"Sweetheart, I can tell you get anxious when we are debating or discussing our different opinions. It is important for people to talk about what they think and it is rare that everyone will agree about everything. Your Dad and I agree about most of the important things, and we disagree about a few of the important things. When we disagree, I must tell him what I think or he won't understand. He can't read my mind. Since no one can read minds, it is important to tell others when we disagree. By telling others when we disagree and discussing it, we can all learn. This is how most humans learn from each other. Sometimes, people believe things so strongly they raise their voices, but that is just an indication of how much they believe in what they are saying."

Because these children are focused on maintaining their routines and cooperating with others, they may not naturally come up with ideas or new ways of doing things. Parents and teachers can coach these children to further develop their creativity by asking questions such as:

"If you were going to invent a new animal, what kind of an animal would it be? Would it be big or little, soft or fuzzy? What would you name it?"

"If you were going to change something about being a kid, what would you want to change? Maybe kids would have one day a month when they got to be in charge? Maybe kids would be the teachers for a day? Maybe kids would stay up later in the evening?"

"If we could go on a vacation to the jungle, what do you think we would take with us?"

"If you could invent a machine that would help the world, what would the machine do?"

"If you wanted to invent a new food, what would it be?"

In addition to these types of questions, parents and teachers can use simple games such as "How many ideas can you come up with?" The game consists of asking a question and allowing the child a short time period to come up with ideas. The only rule is that all ideas are rewarded and recognized no matter how silly or impractical they are. For example:

Question:
What could you haul in your wagon?
Answers:
Toys, people, mom and dad, ice cream, clouds, a desk, a dog, a cat, snow, books, cups, teddy bears,

clothes, a tire, rocks, leaves, sticks, potato chips, water, air.
Question:
What can you do with a gallon of ice cream?
Answers:
Eat it all, have a party, take a bath in it, melt it, give it to someone, take it to school, make ice cream cones, feed it to the dog, sell it at an ice cream stand, cool off your head, use it on a bruised arm, paint with it on the street.

By using a range of creativity exercises and enjoyable questions, parents and teachers can use humor and silliness to help these children develop openness and comfort with thinking about new ideas.

Because the Soft-spoken, Cooperative children are so focused on cooperating with others, it is vitally important that parents and teachers guide these children toward an understanding of their own self-importance. Adults must continually reinforce the concept that others are important AND the child is just as important. Some affirmations which may be used to esteem the Soft-spoken child's natural behavior while reinforcing the importance of the child are as follows:
"I like your easy-going energy and sometimes you may want to use a different type of energy to make sure that you get your turn."
"I like the way you try to get along with others and sometimes it is important to let others know that you disagree with them."
"I know how hard you work and sometimes it's O.K. to take a break and just play."
"I like your gentle, kind nature and sometimes others may try to take advantage of you because they think you'll give in. So sometimes it is important to be able to say 'no' and mean it."

As you read through the descriptions of the Soft-spoken, Cooperative children, it is important not to judge their behaviors. There is no best behavioral type. Children need to have their natural behaviors esteemed. They need to be guided toward developing more balanced types of behaviors. Parents and teachers who instruct children in learning new behaviors which balance their natural behaviors can be the most powerful force in the children's lives. They are the ones who will affirm children for their natural behaviors so the children learn they are loved for who they are.

7

Cautious, Concerned Children

Pam was delighted to hear the report that her hopes had been confirmed and she was expecting her first child. When she announced the joyful news to her mother, Pam's mother expressed this wish: "Pam, I hope you are lucky enough to have a child who is just like you. You were a joy to raise. You were always a good little girl. You could play by yourself for hours."

The Cautious, Concerned children from Category 4 are frequently referred to as "good children." These children generally listen closely to authority, try hard to do what is correct and follow the rules. Parents and teachers may not be aware that these children focus considerable attention and energy on trying to figure out the correct behavior. Because they often do what is "correct," they may be ignored by parents and teachers who are trying to manage the inappropriate behaviors of other children, as in the following situation:

First Grade Teacher
"Tessa is a very good student. She usually follows directions and completes her work with a minimum of mistakes. I wish I had more students like her."

Parent
"Some days Tessa seems ... well, sort of worried. When she gets ready for school in the morning she seems to have a lot of stomachaches. And every once in a while there are tears over some minor item. It's not like her usual behavior."

First Grade Teacher
"It does sound like she's having a little stress. We've had some classroom disruptions with students fighting recently. That may have bothered her more than I thought. I'll watch what's happening to her more closely. Some days she's so good I hardly notice she's here."

The upset stomach, tears over little things and other types of stress behavior may reveal a Cautious child who is not getting her "peace and tranquillity" need met. Since peace and harmony are paramount in the lives of these children, they may be frightened of the intense emotions which can destroy their inner calm. Anger, hostility, yelling, arguing or any other out of control behavior from parents, teachers or other children is frightening to most children, but Cautious children may be deeply affected by these emotional behaviors. And, although deeply affected, they may not actually reveal the extent of their pain, as they also may fear their own emotions. Just as they do not want to be around angry people, they do not want to be angry. Their own emotions of anger can destroy their inner sense of peace and harmony. The advantage of this behavior is that these children are the natural "peace keepers." They may go to unusual lengths to make sure others are getting their needs met so the situation stays peaceful. The disadvantage is that these children may strive to maintain the peace at the price of their own rights. The situation with Wally and Gene offers an example of this behavior:

Parent
"There's some cake left for dessert. Do you two want to split it?"

Wally
"I get to cut it."

Parent
"Wally, you cut the cake unevenly. One piece is quite a bit larger than the other."

Wally
Complaining loudly, "NO, don't cut it again. I want the big piece. I'm older than he is; I should get a bigger piece!"

Parent
"Wally, settle down and lower your voice. Since you cut the cake, Gene gets to pick first. Gene, which piece of cake do you want?"

Gene
"I'll take the small piece."

Parent
"Are you sure? You can have the larger piece if you want. I seem to remember that you took the small

piece last time. You don't want to let Wally always
have the larger piece, do you?"
Gene
"It's O.K. I don't mind. Wally likes cake more than I
do."

Wally's loud protests about getting the smaller piece of
cake warned Gene that he would risk losing his peace and
harmony to Wally's pending anger. Gene's desire to maintain
his internal harmony motivated him to keep the peace and give
up his right to the larger piece of cake. The parent, in fact, had
some awareness of what was happening, as Wally frequently
got the larger piece. But Gene was not willing to compete for
the cake If Wally is usually pushy and quarrelsome, Gene may
have decided to let Wally have his way in most situations. Gene
doesn't want to have a conflict with Wally. Gene will try to avoid
situations in which Wally becomes angry. In addition, Gene will
try to avoid situations when he is likely to become angry at
Wally. His parents may frequently find Gene seeking his
harmony alone in his room, especially if Wally continues to
compete with him.

A Cautious Child, like Gene, is motivated to maintain his
internal sense of calm. Because of this motivation, he will try to
avoid any type of conflict if at all possible. If parents or teachers
find a Cautious child yelling or arguing, be aware the child has
been pushed to his limits and may need help debriefing the
situation. All children need guidance about how to manage
anger more effectively. But the Cautious child especially needs
to be affirmed for his right to be angry. Anger is a valuable
emotion which gives humans information about what is
happening to them. It is not the anger itself which is
inappropriate, but the behaviors which result from anger. To
punish this child for getting angry only reinforces the child's own
judgment of himself as someone who should not get angry.
Parents and teachers will need to coach their young Cautious,
Concerned children by saying something like:
"I know you were pretty angry at Mark yesterday.
It's O.K. to feel angry. Feeling angry tells you that
something is 'not O.K.' Feeling your emotions is very
important because they give you information.
Sometimes it can be scary to be angry. It may feel like

the anger is bigger than you. Occasionally it might feel like the anger is uncontrollable. These are feelings that everyone feels sometimes. The important thing to understand is what to do when you are angry. Anger is often the emotion which helps us stand up for our rights so that other people don't walk all over us. Let's look at the choices you have when you feel angry. One of your choices is to take a time out and leave the situation until you feel more able to deal with what is happening. Another choice could be to ask for help from an adult. Still another choice is to take a deep breath and tell the other person what is making you angry. You could say, 'When you do _____, (fill in the blank) I get angry; please stop it.' Sometimes it can be very important to tell the other person when you are angry at him. Let's practice this sentence. Imagine that you are playing with someone and they 'take your toy,' what would you say?"

Although these children, like all children, will get angry or hostile, they usually try hard to suppress these emotions. Parents and teachers may not be aware of the importance of guiding these children toward accepting and, sometimes, responding to these emotions because these children usually have such "good behaviors." It may seem counterproductive to guide a well-behaved child toward acting a little more angry at times, but these children must develop more comfort with emotions and learn that emotions, such as anger, are part of being human. By fearing their own anger and the anger of others, these children often give up their rights to keep the peace. Without coaching, these children can give themselves up to avoid conflict, as Jeremy did:

Jeremy was 13 years old when a new neighbor moved in down the street. One morning, while he was walking his normal route to school, Frank, the new 13 year old neighbor, stopped him and decreed: "I live on this street and I don't want you walking here anymore!" Jeremy was angry and both boys yelled at each other for several minutes during the confrontation. The next day Jeremy walked right down the sidewalk next to Frank's house. Frank was on the porch and they yelled at each other. Frank jumped off the porch threatening

Jeremy and Jeremy stood his ground. The same scene was repeated for several mornings. Then Jeremy changed his route. He walked three blocks out of his way to avoid Frank's house. Jeremy was satisfied that he wasn't a coward. By standing up to Frank for a week, Jeremy had proven to himself he could stand his ground. But the continual anger was destroying his peaceful walk to school, so he changed routes. He had to start earlier and walk further, but it was worth it to preserve his quiet morning.

Jeremy may have made the best choice. But if he'd brought the situation to the attention of parents or teachers, he may have gotten some coaching with alternative ways of handling the situation. There may be times in Jeremy's life that walking the extra blocks to avoid the conflict is the best alternative. But Jeremy must also learn when not to walk the extra blocks and when to demand his right to walk on a public street without being harassed. Children like Jeremy need to be guided toward understanding their options in situations. There are other options besides daily conflict with Frank or walking the extra blocks.

Frequently, these children will see only two options in situations: acquiesce or engage in conflict. Engaging in conflict means they risk: 1. getting angry, 2. having to deal with someone else's anger or 3. getting in trouble. These children understand the rules for children which can be stated: "No fighting, no yelling, no arguing or unpleasant conflicts and if there's a conflict everyone will be punished." It's obvious the Cautious child will be motivated to acquiesce since he is afraid of anger and wants to follow the rules. Sometimes, even the best efforts of the Cautious child will not keep him from getting in trouble, as in the case of Paul:

Ten year old Paul was playing soccer with friends in his backyard. There were several wasps buzzing as they kicked the ball toward the house. John, one of Paul's friends, stopped kicking the ball and turned toward the boys.

"Hey, look guys, there's a wasp nest up there next to the roof," called John.

"My dad says he's going to get rid of it this weekend," responded Paul.

John immediately decided, "I bet we could do it for him!"

"I don't think we should do anything. My Dad says the wasps can be dangerous. Maybe we should go play in the front yard," Paul tried desperately to distract John.

"We're gonna fix those old wasps." commanded John.

Paul, trying to be enthusiastic pleaded, "Come on John, let's play soccer."

"No way!" declared John. "I'm gonna be a wasp buster."

The other boys began catching John's excitement. They started laughing and joining in. "Yeah, we can be the Wasp Busters."

"There's a garden hose. Let's spray the wasp nest. That'll fix them," chortled John, as the other boys snickered.

"Water will make the wasps mad, John." Paul tried to reason with John. "You don't want the wasps mad. Please John, turn off the water."

Suddenly there were wasps and water everywhere as the nest came down with a dull thud on the back steps. John, still holding the hose, was spraying water in every direction as the wasps attacked anything that moved.

"John, you shithead!" exploded Paul.

By the time he found his mother, Paul was almost hysterical. Paul knew the rules, but couldn't get anyone to enforce them or listen to him. By getting angry at John, Paul lost his internal harmony. By letting John spray the wasps, Paul figured he would get in trouble with his father. No matter what he did, Paul lost his peaceful sense of well-being. Paul's mother interpreted his hysterics as "being afraid that he would be punished." But Paul, like many Cautious children, was misunderstood. All he wanted to do was follow the rules and maintain his internal sense of calm. Paul was upset because he lost his temper, because John sprayed the wasps, because the rules had been broken and because he lost his sense of peace.

If Paul's mother watches carefully, she may see Paul's relationship with John change slightly. John may be asked to play only when other adults are around. Or, Paul may only play with John at the public playground. Or, Paul may prefer to play alone or read, rather than asking all the neighborhood children, including John, to his backyard. Paul probably won't consciously shun John, because it's against his rules of how to get along. But Paul will attempt to keep John from executing a repeat performance and stealing his sense of peace.

These children are often known as the "thinkers" of the four behavioral categories because of the vast amount of time they spend considering how to live life correctly. They ponder how to avoid irritating others. They reflect on what they should do to cause the least disturbance to others, because they know that disturbing others means a conflict and a potential loss of inner calm. In the following illustration, seven year old Debbie has already thought about how to manage her three year old sister.

Father
"Debbie, I know when you come home from school you are tired and want to be alone. But Johanna is usually waiting anxiously at the door for you. What do you do?"

Debbie
"Oh, Dad. I find her something to do, then she leaves me alone."

Father
"How did you know to do that? Did your Mom help you?"

Debbie
"No one helped me. I guess I thought it up by myself."

Cautious children, like Debbie, continually gather information so that they can figure out how to handle situations which disrupt their lives. These children are seekers of information. They listen to stories and accumulate knowledge so that they can distill the "experience" and learn from it. At a very young age, they will start to use their accumulated knowledge to determine the correct action they should take in any given situation. For example, five year old Stan had been watching *Sesame Street* for a few months when he tried his new-found knowledge out on his parents.

Mother

> "Stan, I know you liked the ice cream, but it's not O.K. to lick your plate. Licking your plate is not acceptable table manners."

Stan

> "Mother, you have to realize that we are different. It's alright for people to be different and do different things. Some people just have different ways of doing things."

Stan's parents were stunned when they heard their five year old spouting this information. Stan listened carefully, processed the information, distilled the experience and was attempting to use his *Sesame Street* learnings. These types of experiences with Cautious children often lead parents to wonder if their child is a mini-adult.

Parents and teachers may see these children as reserved and passive because their "thinking" is not observable. Be assured these children are observing, storing information and thinking the majority of the time. They usually have thought through the reasons for almost everything they do, as in the following example:

Father

> "Why do you put your favorite doll in the box she came in when you finish playing with her?"

Child

> "I don't want her to get dirty or hurt and I don't want anyone to see her. If I put her in the toy box she'd rub against the other toys and get dirty. When other kids come to play, she's in the box under my bed and they don't see her so I don't have to share her and risk having her get hurt."

According to their ages, these children can be good at solving some of their own problems. Parents and teachers can often turn a potential crisis into a learning experience by encouraging Cautious children to come up with solutions they like. For example, each morning was turning into a crying session for six year old Edie. The crying was usually about missing the bus. Her mom always walked Edie to the bus. Sonja, who was only two years old, had to be dressed and ready to leave as well. Sonja was the problem. It was fairly predictable for Sonja to struggle with her mom over what clothes to wear. Then Sonja would refuse to walk fast. Instead, the more Edie encouraged Sonja to hurry, the more she slowed down. By the time they reached the bus, Edie was usually in tears, fearful that she'd missed it. She was afraid of breaking two of the important rules: Be on time and don't miss the bus. Finally, her mother decided something had to change.

Mother
> "Edie, I'm tired of all the tears in the morning before school. Even though you have never missed the bus, I know you are afraid that you will. I want you to think about what it will take for you to be comfortable in the morning."

Edie
> "I don't know."

Mother
> "I want you to think about it. Here are some ideas you can consider. Maybe you could walk to the bus with Julie. She's three years older and we could ask her to pick you up in the morning. Maybe we could leave a few minutes early. The bus comes at 8:30. We only walk a block to the corner. We normally leave at 8:20. You think about it and tell me what you want."

Edie
> After thinking for several hours, "Mother, I want to leave early."

Mother
> "How early? Is five minutes earlier enough time?"

Edie
> "No. Ten minutes."

Mother
> "O.K., you've got it. Ten minutes earlier. We'll leave at 8:10. That means we'll be sure to be there when the bus comes."

This solution worked. The first morning they left early Sonja immediately dawdled at the front step. Big sister Edie, smiling at her mother over Sonja's head, said, "Come on Sonja, hurry up or I'll miss the bus." Sonja had all the time in the world to dawdle and Edie could maintain her sense of calm. Edie's mother reports that the extra 10 minutes are well worth the happy faces.

It should come as no surprise to parents and teachers that Cautious children need guidance: in accepting and understanding their feelings, in sharing their knowledge with others, in deciding when not to figure out things, in reframing their understanding of the rules and in developing the ability to be close to others while standing up for themselves.

As parents and teachers will attest, children have strong feelings. They are able to be angry and wail indignantly at the top of their lungs. They are able to show caring and love at an early age. Cautious, Concerned children often connect strong feelings with being bad. Strong feelings such as anger, grief, joy and even love can be experienced as internally overwhelming for the Cautious child. Remember, anything which steals this child's internal sense of calmness can be seen as "bad." Parents and teachers usually reinforce this judgment of strong emotions as wrong, as illustrated in the following examples:

A common adult reaction to an angry child who is acting out his anger toward his sister is: "Stop that! You shouldn't be angry at your sister."

In happy situations, such as a birthday party with children laughing and playing, you may hear a parent or teacher say: "Settle down! You're getting too loud. If you want to continue playing this game you must stop the screaming when someone wins a point."

When a child experiences the grief of a loss, whether it is the loss of a favorite toy or the loss of a friend, a parent may say: "Oh, Honey, please don't cry. I'll show you how we can handle this together. But first you must stop crying."

A child who wants to show love for his mother may want to sit in her lap and cuddle and an unaware parent may say: "Oh, you're getting too big for this," or "You're too heavy; go play with your brother," or "You're getting too old for this behavior."

From all these messages and more, the Cautious child's natural tendency to shy away from strong emotions is so reinforced that the child often tries to stop feeling the strong emotions which are "wrong."

Parents and teachers need a four step approach to guiding their Cautious children through the maze of emotions. First, they need to help their children understand the difference between "feeling the emotion" and "acting on the emotion." Second, parents and teachers need to help their children identify their emotions. Third, adults need to reinforce the importance of "feeling our emotions." Fourth, Cautious children need coaching in what to do when they are feeling strong emotions.

Parents and teachers have many day-to-day opportunities to guide these children toward separating emotions from the actions which may result from them. Adults can help children separate emotions from actions and reinforce the need for feeling emotions by explaining:

"It's O.K. to feel the emotion, but it's not O.K. to take an action which hurts someone else. Human beings have strong emotions. Emotions such as anger or fear tell us when situations are unsafe. Emotions such as joy and love tell us when situations are safe and happy. Emotions are very valuable. They let us know what is happening. When something is wrong people often feel angry. The anger is a signal."

Especially when disciplining these children, parents and teachers must distinguish between the emotion and the action, as Willa's mother did in the following example:

Three year old Anne and Willa were playing with shovels and pails on the beach as their mothers watched. Anne reached over and grabbed Willa's pail. Willa grabbed the handle and started yelling. Anne overpowered Willa and captured the pail. Angrily crying, Willa tried to reach her pail. Anne, undaunted, pushed Willa in the sand. The mothers intervened.

"Anne, you have a time-out. It's not O.K. to push Willa or to take her pail," said Anne's mother.

"Willa, I can see you are angry at Anne for pushing you and taking your pail. Being angry when someone does something unfair is good. I'm also pleased that you didn't hit Willa," said Willa's mother.

Had Willa hit Anne, Willa's mother could have said: "Willa it's O.K. to be angry because Anne took your pail; it's not O.K. to hit someone when you are angry. Because you hit Willa, you have a time-out."

In common everyday situations, parents and teachers can reinforce the importance of "feeling the emotions" while separating out the inappropriate actions which may result from the emotions. In addition to encouraging Cautious children to feel their strong emotions, adults need to help these children identify their emotions.

Because these children may naturally attempt to repress their strong emotions, they may not be aware of their emotional experiences. Alert parents and teachers can help these children identify and honor their emotions by saying things like:

"Tammy, can you tell me how you felt when Bob said you didn't do it right? I noticed you frown. What were you feeling?"

"John, what happened back there? Everyone was just talking and then you got very quiet. What was happening inside you?"

"When she slammed the door and ran out, I felt my stomach start to ache. What did you feel?"

One of the best ways adults can help these children understand how to deal with strong emotions is to model healthy methods of handling emotional situations. For example:

Father talking to child

"Your mom and I had an argument. Sometimes people who love each other argue. When people argue it doesn't mean they don't love each other. Your mom and I love each other and we can still argue now and then."

Adult talking to child

"I'm really feeling angry now. I don't want to do anything that I'll regret later so I'm going to take a time-out."

An additional example of modeling is set forth in the following dialogue between two parents.

Father

"I want to discuss this with you. However, I feel myself getting angry about your treatment of me. I feel put-down. I'll be willing to talk about this later, but not now."

Mother

"I feel angry too. I wasn't putting you down. And I think you're trying to dodge the discussion by saying you'll talk about it later. When will we talk about it?"

Father

"Oh, all right. Let's go out to lunch tomorrow and discuss this. But I want you to listen to what I want to do."

Mother

"I want you to hear me! Then we'll decide together. I think lunch is a good idea. We'll be less likely to yell at each other at a restaurant. But I want to know what will happen if we can't agree."

Teachers often have the opportunity to help Cautious children understand how to manage strong emotions, as in the following example:

Teacher talking to her class

"I'm sorry I slammed the door and yelled at everybody in the classroom. I know that some of you were not the ones who were causing the problems. I was angry. It was unfair to those of you who were trying to read. The students who were causing the trouble have admitted being responsible for the damage. I'm sorry I didn't listen to everyone's side before I kept everyone after school."

When an adult admits to a momentary loss of control and apologizes, it becomes an example to the Cautious child that: it's O.K. to feel strong emotions and if you have a momentary loss of control, you won't be condemned for life. The Cautious child, who is usually gathering information and distilling the experience, will learn much from these types of situations.

Cautious children need guidance in sharing their knowledge with others. They will be more comfortable sharing their knowledge with one or two individuals at a time. In a group of people, these children will be less likely to explain their ideas or thoughts. In groups, there is usually competition for attention, for who can talk the most, for whose ideas are chosen, for who gets the teacher's compliments. Remember, these children do not like to compete. In addition, these children think that their ideas can be attacked more readily in a group. From experience, these children know that there is less safety for them in groups, so their cautious nature emerges and they may not say anything.

For example, a teacher talking privately to Betty said, "I noticed that you didn't say anything when you were with your project group. I know you have good reasons for being quiet. I also know you usually have good ideas to contribute."

Betty, a third grader, responded, "Everyone talked at once. Every time I started to say something someone interrupted me. I don't like being interrupted so I didn't think it was right for me to interrupt someone else ... so I finally decided to just listen."

"But you had some good ideas, didn't you?" asked the teacher.

"Well, I think so," hesitated Betty. "At least I had some ideas that no one else mentioned."

"Don't you think it's important for your ideas to be heard by the group?" coached the teacher.

"I honestly think they'd rather be telling their ideas than listening to mine," said Betty candidly.

"Umm. You may be right. But, I think it is important for you to make sure your ideas are heard. Let's talk about what you could do to stand up for your rights. In a group, you do have a right to have your ideas heard," guided the teacher.

The teacher was able to coach Betty in sharing her ideas and in understanding when to stand up for her rights in groups. These are important concepts for Cautious children to learn. When coaching these children about their interactions, acknowledge their discomfort in groups by saying things like:

"I know that talking in groups can be uncomfortable. Just because you're uncomfortable, it doesn't mean that you should be quiet. Being uncomfortable isn't a 'stop sign.' Many people think that when they feel uncomfortable they should just stop. But sometimes being uncomfortable is a 'GO sign.' That uncomfortable feeling is telling you to stand up for yourself and make sure you are heard."

"I know it's sometimes hard to talk in a group. Sometimes people don't talk because they're afraid that others will disagree with them. If you start to stop yourself from saying something because you're afraid people will disagree with you, remember that you have a right to your own ideas. Just because someone doesn't agree with you, it doesn't mean you're wrong. You have a right to your ideas no matter what anyone thinks. This is one of your most important rights; your right to your own thoughts and ideas. Sometimes people will like your ideas. Sometimes people will not like your ideas. The ideas are still yours."

Groups are rather intimidating to these Cautious children. When first grader Diedre Adams had to walk in front of the whole lunch room to pick up her lunch tray and her milk, she became so nervous she could hardly speak. While visiting her school, Diedre's mother noticed her discomfort and told her:

"Diedre, I noticed that you had to walk in front of the whole lunch room when you got your tray and milk. Some people might feel a little nervous about being in front of the fifth and sixth graders and doing things correctly. I'm so proud of how brave you are. I noticed that even though you were uncomfortable you were able to get your tray and your milk. That's being brave. I'm proud of you. I also want you to know that if something happened, if you forgot to pick up your milk or if you had trouble with your tray, you could go to one of the teachers and they would help you."

Diedre beamed when her mother told her she was proud of her bravery because it was true. For a Cautious child to be in front of a group takes considerable courage!

When coaching Cautious children on how to maintain their rights in groups, be sure to encourage them to take their time and observe what is happening before they offer their ideas. Actually, this is the natural behavior of Cautious children. In most group situations, they will stand back and observe before getting involved with the group activity. They are taking their time to figure out what the norms of the group are, how safe the group is, what is expected of them and much more. So a parent or teacher wouldn't have to encourage them to do this behavior. But, by encouraging them to take their time, the parent or teacher offers these children a comfortable process in an uncomfortable situation. By honoring their natural process and not pushing them into "talking immediately," a behavior which is unnatural for them, parents and teachers allow the child to progress according to his natural motivations. Thus, the whole process becomes more comfortable and manageable for the child.

Cautious Children may appear to make decisions more slowly than other children because they do not want to make a decision. They want to make the correct decision! What adults cannot see is the amount of thinking they generate to make the correct decision. What adults frequently can see is "perfectionism." Cautious children spend much internal energy figuring out the most correct way to behave. Because of this intense mental energy, these children can wear themselves out. They may need time to process the information they gather. Pressing them to hurry only makes it more difficult for them and results in making them feel a loss of self-esteem for being slow, as in the situation with Jennifer.

Her grampa told Jennifer she could pick one doll from the hundreds of dolls in the toy store. Jennifer stood before the dolls and thought.

Her father said, "Jennifer, you always have difficulty making choices. So you have ten minutes to make a choice and if you don't choose then I'll pick a doll for you."

Jennifer didn't say anything. She looked around at the hundreds of dolls with panic in her eyes. She ran to a doll and picked it up. Then she carefully put it back on the shelf and touched another doll's hair. Her entire body was tense with the enormity of deciding which doll was the correct choice from hundreds of wonderful dolls.

Jennifer's grandmother, seeing her granddaughter's dilemma, came to her rescue. "Jennifer, you have enough time to choose. You don't have to hurry." Jennifer's shoulders relaxed visibly. "Now," said her grandmother "do you want a baby doll or a fashion doll?"

"I don't know ..." said Jennifer hesitantly.

"Let's start with baby dolls. Do you have a baby doll at home?" asked her grandmother.

"Oh, yes!" replied Jennifer, catching on to this new way of processing information. "Since I already have three baby dolls, I want to look at fashion dolls."

Jennifer had much to think about. To choose the best doll from hundreds must have been an overwhelming task for her. First she had to figure out her criteria for "best." Was it the doll's clothing, nationality, size, hair style, price or some other unusual factor which would qualify the doll as the "best choice?"

To recover from the intensity of gathering and processing information, these children will need private time. Time away from others' demands and input. Time which allows them to play quietly and think. One young girl unknowingly divulged how much energy it took to process and gather her information.

Mother

"Carol, while you were at school, Hillary's mom called and asked you to go to Colorado with them on a vacation. They want to be sure that Hillary has a good friend to play with while they spend time at their condo. She said they have a swimming pool and horses. What do you think?"

Carol

"How long would it be?"

Mother

"Two weeks. When you went to sixth grade camp last year for a week that was the longest you'd been away from home. Do you think two weeks is too long? Why don't you think about it and we'll talk after dinner."

Carol (after dinner).
"Mom, I've thought about it and would you tell
Hillary's mom that I can't go."
Mother
"I know you have good reasons for your decisions.
Can you tell me your thoughts about this?"
Carol
"Well, it's kinda hard to explain. I like Hillary. She's
my best friend. I like spending the night with her. I
like it when she spends the weekend with us. I like
it when we go to her cabin and spend the weekend
at the lake. But, Hillary is always busy. And,
Hillary's mom is always talking. And, Hillary's
brother is always teasing me. The whole family is
always together. And, the little baby is always
wanting attention. Don't get me wrong. I like it. It's
just that I get tired. I never get to be alone and I get
so tired that when I go to sleep my mind won't shut
off. I keep thinking about all the things that
happened and what people said. Even when I
sleep, I dream about it. Two weeks without being
alone to play or read seems like a long time. Two
weeks of being with Hillary's whole family .... I'd
have so much to think about. I'd be stuffed."

For parents and teachers who do not have a high need
for private time, their Cautious child's motivation to be alone
may be puzzling. It is important to honor the child's need for
privacy and space. Parents of Cautious children often miss the
privacy cues. These children can be subtle in getting this need
met. For example, they may close out the world with a book. It
will appear that they are engaging with the family, but actually
they are physically sitting with the family while, through the
vehicle of reading a book, they are mentally creating their own
internal private space. These children may be drawn to books,
not only because they like gathering information and
experiences, but also because it affords them private space.

The privacy need can be observed in sensitive
situations when these children refuse to tell parents or teachers
what they are thinking. When adults ask personal questions or
somehow engage in behaviors which invade private and

personal space, these children may act out their displeasure. An example of this occurred when an aunt gave a birthday present of panties to her eight year old niece. The niece was privately embarrassed by the gift but wouldn't tell anyone. To tell someone would mean she was embarrassed twice: once when she opened the gift in front of everyone and, once when she revealed her embarrassment. When her mother asked her if she was uncomfortable with the gift, the child merely said, "I don't want to talk about it." Her mother pushed the issue by saying, "I think you might have been embarrassed, but you shouldn't be embarrassed." Of course, the daughter exploded, "I told you I wouldn't talk about it. I'll never talk to you again."

The Cautious child needs to have quiet time to process the information he has gathered. In schools, finding quiet time may be almost impossible. Frequently, the classroom is geared for activity. In the flurry to get to the next subject, the Cautious child often is at a loss to find the time and space to think about what he just learned.

Because the Cautious child spends so much time processing, he may try to figure out everything. Parents and teachers need to guide the child toward processing information which is a priority in their lives and not trying to figure out everything. Under stress, these children may be driven to concentrate on even the lowest priority as they try to figure out the correct thing to do, as in the following situation.

Child

"Mom, when I go to first grade next year, what will happen if the teacher tells me to do something and I don't understand? ... What will happen if the bus doesn't show up? ... What will happen if the bus is late? ... What will happen if the teacher doesn't let us catch the bus? ... What will happen if they run out of food for lunch? ... What if I forget my lunch? ... What if I have to go to the bathroom and the teacher won't let me?"

Because of some stress in his life, this child was clearly concerned about how he would figure out first grade, even though the start of the school year was still months away. Parents and teachers can guide these children into "letting go" of spending exhausting mental energy figuring out situations which are unpredictable by saying things like:

Parent

"Sometimes we can spend time figuring out things and they still don't work out like we planned. That's part of being human. Sometimes you can do your very best and things still are unpredictable. In those cases we just do what we can do. It's important to decide which things you can figure out and which things you can't and let go of the ones you can't. What you can trust is that your mom and I are here to help you."

One way to help these children use their figuring out energy more creatively is to focus their attention on planning low-risk options in scary situations. These children need to know there is a "way out" if things get out of control or if they are feeling out of control. Teachers may be able to offer these children a break from the intense school day by saying: "If things are really feeling out of control for you, you may take a five minute break and sit quietly before continuing." Parents may want to say: "Here's my telephone number. If it is very serious and things seem out of control, you can always call me and I will come and pick you up." It is unlikely that these children will take the parents and teachers up on their offers, but if they do it is important to listen to their fears. Whatever "way out" parents and teachers choose to use with these children, it is important to understand that the adults are providing a safety net so that these children see the situations as more low-risk.

Because these children are motivated to follow the rules, they may end up giving up their rights and themselves. To these children the rule of "no fighting" may mean that they must give up their dessert to keep the classroom bully from creating a conflict. Parents and teachers need to reframe the child's understanding of the rules with the child as an equally important part of the picture; the rules are important AND the child's rights are just as important. These children will need careful coaching as to when it is O.K. to break the rules. Some examples of this type of coaching might sound like:

"Yes, you should usually follow the directions of an adult, but if you feel that the adult is 'wrong,' you can break that rule. For example if an adult touches you and it feels 'bad', you should say, 'Leave me alone' and then tell me or your dad about it."

"The rules are important, but you are just as important as the rules. I know one of the rules is not to fight, but if someone hits you, you have the right to defend yourself by hitting back."

"I know the rule is not to interrupt, but in groups when everyone interrupts, you may choose to interrupt to get your ideas heard."

As you complete reading about the Cautious, Concerned children, it is important that you do not label or judge their behaviors as good or bad. Each behavioral style has strengths and weaknesses. There is no best behavioral category. Every child needs to be guided toward building on his strengths and developing new behaviors to minimize his weaknesses. It is critical that children are affirmed for their natural behaviors so that they learn they are accepted and loved for who they are. Some sentences which affirm the Cautious children are:

"I like you just as you are. I like your thoughtful energy. I'm glad that you are cautious. I like the way you are attentive to what others say. It's O.K. to take your time and do things well."

8

Don't Take it Personally

The two children danced into the room with noise and laughter. Banging skates, slamming doors, high-pitched giggles, rosy cheeks and a whoosh of cold air accompanied them into the front hallway.

"Dad, guess what? I learned how to skate backwards. You should have seen me. I was great," chattered the most rosy-cheeked of the children.

"How many times have I told you not to slam that door? And you're dripping water all over the floor. Did you mark the wall with your skate? There's a cut in the wallpaper right there!" exploded their father.

Later, when he had cooled down, the father reported: "I felt embarrassed, even ashamed of myself. I was yelling about slamming doors and small marks on the wall. But my anger didn't have much to do with the children. They were just being children. I was angry for a lot of reasons. I was angry because that's how my parents treated me. I can remember my father yelling at me about the screen door every time I went outside. I was also angry because they were noisy and I wanted a quiet afternoon. They upset my quiet. I got angry because I didn't get what I wanted. I know I have a responsibility to give clear feedback to them about their behavior and slamming the door is usually not O.K. They do need some coaching about the different behaviors which are acceptable outdoors and not O.K. indoors. But, I could have just told them that and given them consequences. I could have still enjoyed their joy. They were so joyful when they came in ... until I got angry. I'm most upset about my anger ... it seems that where my children are concerned ... the volume of my anger is always on loud."

When children get angry, cry, push against the rules, pout, slam doors, laugh or use any of their natural behaviors to get their needs met, parents and teachers often take it personally. Children seem to have an affinity for getting "under the skin" of the adults in their lives. The adults' responses may be the result of: not getting their own needs met, feeling inadequate, experiencing the situation as out of control or believing others will judge them because of the child's behavior. Whatever responses arise, they are usually about the adults' issues. Children do not get up in the morning planning how to get parents and teachers angry. Yet the child may naturally behave in such a way as to touch the most sensitive issues of the adults. A parent who wants to be in control of her environment may explode in anger when a child starts to act out. A teacher who wants his own sense of calm and tranquillity may severely discipline a child who creates excitement in her life. In order to guide and coach children effectively, teachers and parents need to develop an understanding of themselves: how they are motivated and why they behave as they do. It's not enough to know why children do what they do; the adults must also know themselves. The best coaching will occur when the adults have an understanding of both the children's behaviors and their own. Parents and teachers need to understand why they take their children's behaviors so personally. They need to ask questions about their own lives; questions like: "What do I need?" "What do I believe?" and "Who am I?" The answers to these questions are frequently hidden in the memories of their own childhood, their past experiences, their own natural behaviors and their own fears. For the parents and teachers who are willing to face themselves and look at their own life journeys, they may find the answers they seek by reading the book, *Real Self: The Inner Journey of Courage.*[2] *Real Self* asks parents and teachers to look at their role in the parent-child equation.

As this book comes to an end, may the parents and teachers who read it come to a beginning; a beginning of a new understanding of the children in their lives.

---

2. More information about *Real Self: The Inner Journey of Courage* is available on page 118.

Other books and programs written by Sandra Merwin

REAL SELF: THE INNER JOURNEY OF COURAGE, is a gentle, demanding book. It offers you a road map ot the inner journey and asks you to face yourself, free your dragons and be real. You'll find a new language for answering the questions: "What do I need?" "What do I believe?" and "Who am I?" You'll discover that you are the world's best expert on yourself. You'll have the opportunity to answer "life-changing" questions about yourself. Best of all, you'll gain a language to narrate your own story.

SANDRA MERWIN SPEAKS is an audio album which addresses how you can develop a deeper, richer relationship with yourself. Each cassette contains approximately an hour of gentle teaching stories, quiet contemplative images and bold questions which will allow you to listen to the quiet voice of your highest self.

The *REAL SELF STUDY PROGRAM* is designed to touch both the hearts and minds of your participants. This flexible 12 week program was developed especially for adult study groups. The book, *REAL SELF: THE INNER JOURNEY OF COURAGE*; the audio album, *SANDRA MERWIN SPEAKS* and the step-by-step LEADERS GUIDE support and counsel participants as they discover the answers they seek. The program uses a range of techniques including individual reflections, group exercises, handouts, discussion questions and self-assessment tools.

SAFE IN THE STREETS uses a direct practical approach (based on real-life stories of people who successfully prevented or stopped attacks) to illustrate the range of behaviors possible in any given situation and to reinforce the message: "You can take charge of your own life and safety."

RESOURCES

To obtain the instruments mentioned in this book, contact your local Carlson Learning Network Associate or Carlson Learning Company, Carlson Parkway, P.O. Box 59159, Minneapolis, Minnesota 55459-8247, (612) 449-2856

Other recommended materials from Carlson Learning Company:

The Mysteries of Motivation by Michael O'Connor and Sandra Merwin

The Values Conflict Action Planner by Michael O'Connor and Sandra Merwin

The Classical Styles Audio Album by Michael O'Connor and Sandra Merwin

FOR MORE INFORMATION ABOUT:

• Sandra Merwin's other books and programs

• Quantity discounts for bulk purchases of this book

Contact:

TigerLily Press
4655 Baker Road
Minnetonka, MN. 55343